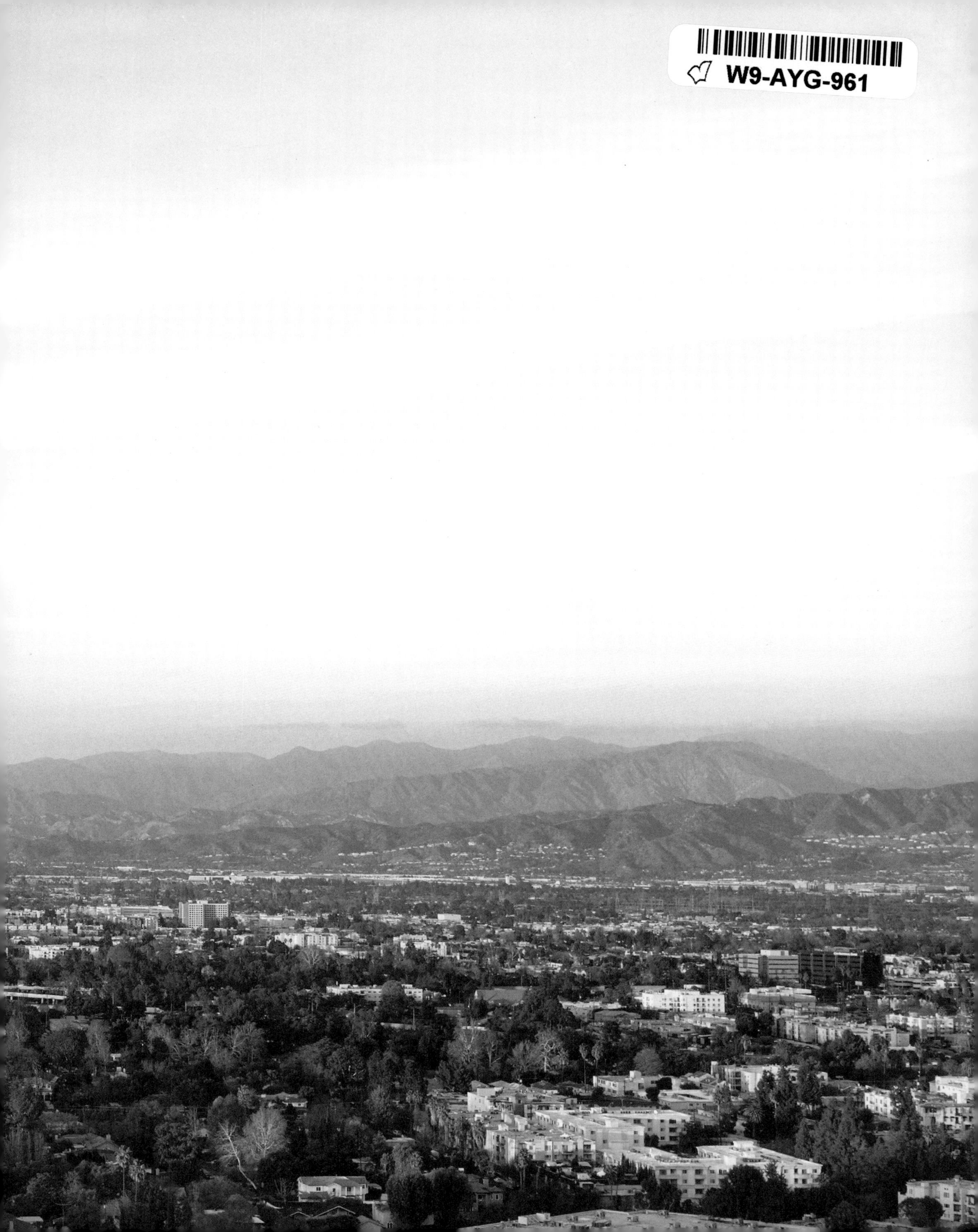

VALERIE'S
HOME COOKING

VALERIE'S
HOME COOKING

More than **100** Delicious Recipes
to Share with Friends and Family

VALERIE BERTINELLI

Oxmoor
House®

Published by Oxmoor House, an imprint of Time Inc. Books
225 Liberty Street, New York, NY 10281

Editorial Director: Anja Schmidt
Assistant Editor: April Smitherman Colburn
Project Editor: Lacie Pinyan
Design Director: Melissa Clark
Photo Director: Paden Reich
Designer: Allison Chi
Text: with Todd Gold
Recipes and Food Photography: Time Inc. Food Studios
Cover and Lifestyle Photography: Brian Bowen Smith
Stylist: Alicia Buszczak
Food Stylist: Alyse Sakai
Wardrobe: Lori Eskowitz-Carter
Retouching: Martina Tolot
Hair and Makeup: Lisa Ashley and Kim Urgel
Assistant Production Director: Sue Chodakiewicz
Senior Production Manager: Greg A. Amason
Copy Editor: Dolores Hydock
Proofreader: Donna Baldone
Indexer: Mary Ann Laurens

ISBN-13: 978-0-8487-5228-6

Scholastic Softcover
ISBN-13: 978-0-8487-5659-8

Signed version
ISBN-13: 978-0-8487-5664-2

Library of Congress Control Number: 2017939646

First Edition 2017
Printed in China
10 9 8 7 6 5 4 3 2 1

We welcome your comments and suggestions about Time Inc. Books.

Time Inc. Books
Attention: Book Editors
P.O. Box 62310
Tampa, Florida 33662-2310

Time Inc. Books products may be purchased for business or promotional use.
For information on bulk purchases, please contact Christi Crowley in the
Special Sales Department at (845) 895-9858.

CONTENTS

COME ON INTO MY KITCHEN

Twenty-five years ago, people came up to me and asked for an autograph. These days, I still get recognized when I go out, but more often than not, I'm asked for a recipe, and I'm fine with that change. Actually, I love it. Playing Barbara Cooper on *One Day at a Time,* as I did in the 1970s, or more recently, Melanie Moretti on *Hot in Cleveland,* came with certain expectations that could be hard to live up to. The role of a home cook is much more comfortable. It's the real me.

To know me, in fact, is to spend time with me in the kitchen. I come from a family of artists, and the kitchen is where I express myself, where I am truly at home. Under the watchful eyes of five cats and a dog, I pull my hair back, roll up my sleeves, and pull out ingredients from the fridge. I follow recipes. I also experiment. I like the process of chopping and mixing. I taste constantly. I occasionally toss a mistake in the sink. And I enjoy the feeling I get from sharing something I love. It's my favorite way of connecting with family and friends.

At this stage of my life, my son is grown and I am reaping the benefits of deep, long friendships with moms I have known since our children were in kindergarten. I get the most pleasure from sharing experiences and creating new ones, and they're always better when I fill the table with delicious food. My home reflects these passions. The kitchen is light and airy, like a painter's studio except there are pots and pans instead of canvasses, and my backyard includes a vegetable garden, a corner where we grow herbs, fruit trees, and even a vineyard on the side of a broad, sloping hill.

I'm open to inspiration. Finding a vine of ripe tomatoes in the garden makes me think of whipping up a panzanella. While picking lemons off the trees in my backyard, I hear a debate in my head:

"Salmon or lemon bars? Or even Limoncello?" Ideas can come from a note I have written myself ("fennel and figs?"), a photo on my phone reminding me of a meal my husband, Tom, and I had on our last road trip, or seeing a bunch of fresh basil at a farmers' market.

COOKING IS IN MY DNA

While traveling in Italy several years ago, I learned my great-grandmother was a cook in a summer home and sold her homemade gelato in her tiny village in order to make enough money to emigrate to America. As a little girl, I spent countless hours in my grandmother's basement kitchen, watching her make homemade pasta, as the other women in the family helped and told stories. As far as I'm concerned, our family history is inseparable from her gnocchi and capelletti.

My mother's specialty was Italian food, even though she's of English-Irish descent and raised in New Jersey. She learned to cook from the women in my father's family. When I was a kid, she made a mean lasagna, and the rich, creamy goodness of her risotto still races to the forefront of my mind when I think of perfection at the end of a fork.

I loved cooking for my son, Wolfie, and whenever work took me away from home, I thought about the special meals I would make when I got back. Indeed, once back home, I eagerly returned to being a mom, which meant carpools and kitchen duty. No one made meatloaf with more purpose or enthusiasm than me. Now, I relish the time Tom and I spend together in the kitchen, alone or entertaining family and friends.

My passion for sharing what I love inspired my TV show, *Valerie's Home Cooking*. In 2013, Tom and I returned from an amazing trip to Italy and suggested a series where we shared our experience traveling and eating fabulous meals. After listening to me talk about food and the way I tried to re-create these incredible meals at home, the executives at the Food Network suggested a home cooking show instead. I waited all of fifteen seconds before saying, "Yes, I'd love to do it." I knew it was the right decision when they came up with the name of my show, *Valerie's Home Cooking*. It captured me—and now, after six seasons, I can confidently say it's everything I'm about right now.

RECIPES FOR THE HEART AND SOUL

The recipes in this book are like that, too. I personally selected every single one in this book. I created some and acquired others from family and friends, including my mother. All of them share two ingredients that are essential to me: heart and soul. Even the simplest recipes here, like Sloppy Joes, evoke a warm feeling in me, and my hope is they have the same effect on you. Over the years, I have served everything in this book at home for casual get-togethers and special occasions. I've improved on the recipes to the point where they're ready to share, and I'm very excited about this opportunity to hopefully help and inspire you.

I'm assuming we are a lot alike, in that when I'm cooking for family, friends, my book club, or a party, or if I'm just preparing a grocery list for the week, I look through my magazines and cookbooks for ideas. There are a lot of yummy ideas here and they are intended for people like you and me, home cooks. They are organized into chapters that reflect the way I think of meals, along with the variables like whether it's Tuesday morning and you're getting a late start versus a leisurely Sunday brunch with family. To me, lunch is more about what I need to get through the rest of the day than a three-course sit-down, starting at twelve or one. I added suggestions for Happy Hour—because why not, that's me, too—and you should know the chapters where I've organized entrées, sides, and sweets are personal and family favorites.

Recently, I picked up my mom's wooden recipe box and began going through the index cards with her handwritten recipes. (You will see several in this book.) Some I remembered from my childhood. Some cards were stained; those are the dishes she made all the time. Each recipe was, in a way, like a short story: The roast was for a birthday, the casserole for a family get-together, and the meatloaf for the start of the school year. These are the treasures that get passed down from generation to generation—not just the food but the stories, too. Years from now, I hope the pages in this book are stained from repeated use.

LAST WORDS OF ADVICE

Keep in mind, though, the best part of home cooking is that you do it at home. It's low-pressure, accessible, and all about the one ingredient I can't provide. It's also the most important ingredient of all. It's you. This is what recipes mean when they say "season to taste." Professional chefs are trained to know how a dish is supposed to taste, but even then, the greats rely on their own unique palates. I'm learning what I like, and you will learn what tastes great to you.

Leave yourself enough time to enjoy the process of preparing each course. Get to know your food in its natural, raw state. Feel the texture. Appreciate the differences in your ingredients and pay attention to how they are combined. If you rush, you will miss the nuances that make a home-cooked meal an essential ingredient in the recipe for a happy home. Don't worry about mistakes, either. They happen. One Christmas, my husband grilled a beef tenderloin to perfection. Our guests talked about it for a year. Those same guests are *still* talking about my gravy. Why? Instead of using flour, I stirred in powdered sugar. I'm sure the Hot Toddies had something to do with that.

Inevitably, you put your own spin on every recipe, and that's my favorite part about cooking. It never gets boring. Every dish is a new adventure. Sometimes I eat the same thing three nights in a row because I love it so darn much. Then it's on to a new adventure. There's a story behind every recipe. Indeed, that is true with the recipes in this cookbook. And now it's time for you to create your own stories.

CHAPTER 1

RISE & SHINE

Don't try to pin me down, but I'm pretty sure morning is my favorite time of the day. Every time I think otherwise, I wake up at dawn and think, "Oh, this is so beautiful." True confession, though: I like to go back to sleep if I don't have to go to work. So I'm sort of a morning person and sort of a later-in-the-morning person.

Once up, I love that moment of stepping into the kitchen and inhaling the rich aroma of freshly brewed coffee. As soon as my eyes open in bed, I begin to anticipate that first taste and watching the sun rise. I hold the hot mug close to my face and stare at the vista outside the kitchen window. It's like a meditation.

By cup number two, I'm wide awake and thinking about what to have for breakfast. To me, breakfast is that transition between "I'm up," and "Now I'm going to start my day." Besides vitamins and nutrients, I get to fuel my body with a generous serving of purposeful kindness. I indulge in whatever my body craves. I might have a breakfast sammie three days in a row because it tastes so dang good. Or I might change it up with some muesli or muffins.

Time is the biggest factor in this decision. Sometimes I run late. Other times I linger in my PJs and bathrobe. Then there are special occasions when friends and family come for brunch and I have to get things going quickly. Whatever the variables, my one constant is the satisfaction I get from providing the day with a delicious start. The slate is clean, the day is full of possibilities, and so is the first meal of the day.

It's a priority with me, and I used it to inspire my selections in this chapter. I'm excited about the recipes here. Some are quick and easy, and you can literally make breakfast in the time it takes to brew a cup of coffee. Others are for the weekend, holidays, or when family is in town and you want to spend a leisurely morning cooking and baking. The Steel-Cut Overnight Oatmeal is a favorite when I'm working and my schedule is tightly booked. I'll admit it: I often skip putting it in a bowl and eat it straight from the container I made it in the night before.

You're going to learn something else about me in this chapter. I'm mercurial. I love my bacon, but I also love a nice, healthy smoothie. It really depends on my mood, what my body craves, and where I am at that day. One last note that will stay between us: If you crave breakfast for lunch or dinner, these recipes will still work for you. No matter the time of day, I have found these ensure a good meal.

This is the perfect breakfast for when I'm in a hurry. I add all the ingredients, blend, and it's ready in minutes. But the fresh, healthy way it tastes and jump-starts my energy level at the same time is the real luxury. It's also efficient. I always have frozen bananas on hand. As soon as the bunch I brought home from the market starts to go dark (and I know I'm not going to make banana bread), I slice them up, store them in a baggie, and pop them in the freezer. Voilà, fresh bananas. Since I use coconut milk and almond milk in my coffee, they're also staples in the fridge. The same goes for almond butter. And the coffee in this recipe? Just make an extra cup. You get the idea. This one's easy, it packs a nutritious punch, and it's great to drink on the go.

All-in-One Breakfast Smoothie

SERVES **2**   HANDS-ON **5 MINUTES**   TOTAL **5 MINUTES**

Process the bananas, ice, milk, coffee, oats, honey, almond butter, chopped chocolate-covered espresso beans, coconut oil, and vanilla in a blender until smooth. Pour evenly into 2 glasses. Garnish with the chocolate-covered espresso beans and a sprig of mint, if you wish.

2 ripe bananas, peeled and frozen

1 cup ice

1 cup unsweetened almond milk

½ cup brewed cold-brew coffee

½ cup uncooked regular rolled oats

3 tablespoons honey

2 tablespoons almond butter

2 tablespoons chopped chocolate-covered espresso beans

1 tablespoon coconut oil, melted

1 teaspoon vanilla extract

Chocolate-covered espresso beans, for serving

2 mint sprigs, for serving (optional)

INGREDIENT NOTE
Cold-brew coffee can be found in the dairy section of most grocery stores. Or use chilled leftover coffee or espresso.

MAKE AHEAD
Make this the night before to grab on-the-go in the morning.

4 cups uncooked regular rolled oats

1 cup unsweetened flaked coconut

¼ cup roasted, salted pepitas (shelled pumpkin seeds)

1 cup coarsely chopped roasted, salted almonds

1 cup chopped dried apricots

¼ cup poppy seeds

½ teaspoon ground ginger

¼ teaspoon ground allspice

¼ teaspoon kosher salt

1 cup unsweetened almond milk or whole milk (for 1 serving muesli)

1 tablespoon pure maple syrup or honey (for 1 serving muesli)

▷ VARIATION ◁

Any variety of fruit, nuts, sweeteners, milks, and spices can be used. I frequently use hemp seeds, which are loaded with antioxidants, instead of poppy seeds or the popular chia seeds, which I have a slight allergy to. The world is your oyster!

MAKE AHEAD

The muesli mix can be stored in an airtight container for up to 2 weeks, and you can scoop out portions as needed. Prepare your individual portion the night before to take to work with you in the morning.

I once told someone that I liked a variety of textures in my oatmeal—cereals, dried fruits, nuts, and seeds—and she said, "Oh, then you're talking about muesli." I had no idea, but that's the quick difference: Oatmeal is just that, oatmeal, while muesli is a combination of ingredients, as in this recipe. The first time I had a version of this "overnight muesli," in fact, was on the set of my show, *Valerie's Home Cooking*. It was in our fridge, and my culinary producer was spooning out a serving for herself. "What's that?" I asked. "Muesli," she said. "It's delicious. I made it last night." I tried it and was over the moon. I have since adapted her recipe with my own favorites, which is the beauty of this dish. You fine-tune to your taste or alternate your favorite nuts and dried fruits. It's easy and satisfying.

Overnight Almond-Apricot Muesli

SERVES **8**   HANDS-ON **15 MINUTES**   TOTAL **2 HOURS, 35 MINUTES**

1 Preheat the oven to 350°F. Combine the oats, coconut, and pepitas on a large rimmed baking sheet. Bake until toasted, 5 to 7 minutes. Cool completely, about 20 minutes.

2 Toss together the toasted oat mixture, almonds, apricots, poppy seeds, ginger, allspice, and salt in a large bowl until combined. To prepare 1 serving of the muesli, scoop 1 cup of the mixture into an airtight container; pour the milk over the mixture to cover by ½ inch. Chill 2 hours or overnight. Store the remaining mixture in an airtight container for up to 2 weeks.

3 Serve the muesli chilled, drizzled with the syrup, or microwave the muesli on HIGH until warm, about 2 minutes, and drizzle with the syrup.

Whenever I make oatmeal, I'm reminded of the time I moved from my parents' house into my first apartment. One of the few things I took with me was a box of instant oatmeal from the pantry. I made it every morning. My Steel-Cut Overnight Oatmeal is obviously not instant, but it's quick, simple, and guaranteed to leave you satisfied. I made it on my cooking show for my husband, Tom, though I'm stretching the truth when I say I made it. The slow cooker does all the work. Tom and I both like the options of this breakfast. You can add coconut, berries, bananas—really, anything that you feel like—or you can go with the basics and enjoy the old-fashioned, creamy oatmeal that you grew up on. I alternate between the classic and adding crunch, depending on what I find on my shelves. When I was a kid, sometimes the biggest decision of my day was deciding which flavor oatmeal I wanted in the morning. In that way, this dish brings out the kid in me.

Steel-Cut Overnight Oatmeal

SERVES **8**   HANDS-ON **15 MINUTES**   TOTAL **6 HOURS, 15 MINUTES**

Combine the water, oats, cinnamon stick, nutmeg, and salt in a 6-quart slow cooker. Cook on LOW for 5 to 6 hours. Top the servings with the sliced bananas; sprinkle with the brown sugar, or drizzle with the syrup. Serve with the toasted nuts, toasted coconut, berries, coconut milk, or almond milk.

7½ cups water

1½ cups uncooked steel-cut oats

1 cinnamon stick

½ teaspoon grated fresh nutmeg

⅛ teaspoon kosher salt

2 ripe bananas, sliced

Brown sugar or pure maple syrup, for serving

Toasted nuts, toasted shredded coconut, fresh or dried berries, coconut milk, or almond milk, for serving

EQUIPMENT

You will need a slow cooker for this recipe.

½ cup plus 1 tablespoon coconut oil

2½ cups uncooked regular rolled oats

2½ cups crisp white or brown rice cereal

¾ cup roasted, salted pistachios

¼ cup slivered almonds

1 teaspoon kosher salt

1 teaspoon ground cinnamon

½ teaspoon ground cardamom

½ cup pure maple syrup

1 teaspoon vanilla extract

¾ cup dried tart cherries, chopped

MAKE AHEAD

This recipe can be stored for up to 10 days.

Though granola has been around since the mid 1800s, I first heard about it in the late '60s and early '70s. It was considered healthy and natural, and outdoorsy people were described as "crunchy granola types." Well, not much has changed. I'm a fan of good, homemade granola, the kind whose ingredients, you can tell, have been carefully selected and combined according to desired taste and texture. It can be a morning cereal or a snack later in the day after an invigorating hike. I like this granola for its versatility. Any variety of dried fruit or nuts can be used. Honey can be subbed for the maple syrup. Canola oil can be subbed for the coconut oil. If you're like me, you will find yourself in traffic or lying in bed and suddenly think, "Oh my God, I can use raisins with the dried cherries! Or what about cranberry raisins?" To which I say, "Why not! Go crai-zee."

Slow-Cooker Granola

SERVES **8**   HANDS-ON **30 MINUTES**   TOTAL **3 HOURS, 30 MINUTES**

1 Lightly grease a 5- to 6-quart slow cooker with 1 tablespoon of the coconut oil. Add the oats, rice cereal, pistachios, almonds, salt, cinnamon, and cardamom; stir to combine.

2 Combine the maple syrup, vanilla, and remaining ½ cup coconut oil in a small saucepan. Cook over medium, stirring often, until melted and incorporated. Pour over the oat mixture in the slow cooker, and stir until fully coated. Cover, venting the lid about ¼ inch, and cook on HIGH until toasted and crunchy, 2 to 2 ½ hours, stirring every 30 to 45 minutes.

3 Spread the granola on a parchment paper-lined rimmed baking sheet. Stir in the dried cherries, and cool completely, about 1 hour.

A couple things are going on here. There's the fact that I just plain like muffins. I like the way they smell when they come out of the oven, the way they look on a platter, and of course the way they taste. Then there is my fondness for bananas. This is really a life-long love affair, dating back to when I was a kid and liked bananas on everything from cereal to ice cream sundaes—or by themselves, in their natural state as a quick, nutritious snack. Knowing they are an excellent source of potassium has made them a daily staple in my diet. They're a perfect pick-me-up. And if there is an all-time funniest fruit, it's the banana—and I'm a sucker for a sense of humor. But these muffins are no joke. They're a tasty use for when your bananas start to get overly ripe. They are light, moist, and work wonderfully with blueberries. I like that the combination gives me vitamins and antioxidants first thing in the morning. They also work with any fresh berry.

Blueberry-Banana-Oat Breakfast Muffins

SERVES **12**   HANDS-ON **10 MINUTES**   TOTAL **35 MINUTES**

1 Preheat the oven to 400°F. Generously grease a 12-cup muffin pan. Stir together the flour, oats, sugar, baking powder, salt, and ¾ cup of the blueberries in a medium bowl. Stir together the bananas, butter, egg, and vanilla in a separate bowl. Add the banana mixture to the flour mixture, gently stirring until just blended.

2 Spoon ⅓ cup batter into each prepared muffin cup; top evenly with the remaining ½ cup blueberries.

3 Bake until a wooden pick inserted in the center of the muffin comes out clean, about 18 minutes. Cool in the pan on a wire rack for 5 minutes; remove the muffins from the pan to the wire rack. Serve warm or at room temperature.

1½ cups all-purpose flour

¾ cup uncooked regular rolled oats

½ cup granulated sugar

2 teaspoons baking powder

½ teaspoon kosher salt

1¼ cups fresh blueberries

1 cup mashed ripe bananas (about 2 large bananas)

6 tablespoons unsalted butter, melted

1 large egg, beaten

½ teaspoon vanilla extract

BLUEBERRY-BANANA-
OAT BREAKFAST
MUFFINS
PG 23

CHERRY-COCONUT
SCUFFINS
PG 27

BACON-CARAMEL
SCUFFINS WITH
CARAMEL CLOTTED
CREAM
PG 26

6 bacon slices

1½ cups all-purpose flour

1 teaspoon baking powder

⅛ teaspoon kosher salt

½ cup unsalted butter, softened

½ cup packed light brown sugar

1 large egg

½ teaspoon vanilla extract

½ cup half-and-half

¼ cup jarred caramel sauce

½ cup jarred clotted cream

INGREDIENT NOTE

Clotted cream is a British condiment made simply from aged heavy cream. It's thick, like yogurt, but very rich and delicious.

◆ TRICK TECHNIQUE ◆

More often than not, I crisp my bacon in the oven and not on the stove. Line a baking sheet with foil and set the bacon on a wire rack.

I'm going to level with you. I couldn't decide whether this recipe belonged in this chapter or in the back with the desserts. These scuffins—part scone, part muffin—are so beyond delicious, rich, and decadent they could easily be dessert. But the bacon convinced me to put them here. (I prefer the center cut, by the way. It's nice and thin, there's a little less fat, and it crisps up nicely.) This is one of those breakfasts I make for a celebration with the family or when I want to treat myself like a queen. I created them using mini-muffin tins so more than one can be eaten. I recommend eating them first thing out of the oven. Crack them open and as the steam pours out, spoon in the clotted cream. Then enjoy. With the caramel and bacon together, they have that salty-sweet complexity that always inspires the same reaction: "Oh my goodness." You'll see.

Bacon-Caramel Scuffins with Caramel Clotted Cream

SERVES **12**   HANDS-ON **35 MINUTES**   TOTAL **1 HOUR**

1   Preheat the oven to 350°F. Lightly grease a 24-cup miniature muffin pan.

2   Arrange the bacon in a single layer on a wire rack, and place on an aluminum foil-lined rimmed baking sheet. Bake until very crisp and brown, 30 to 35 minutes. Cool for 10 minutes; finely chop. Leave the oven on 350°F.

3   Meanwhile, stir together the flour, baking powder, and salt in a medium bowl.

4   Beat the butter and brown sugar in a large bowl with an electric mixer at medium speed until light and fluffy, about 2 minutes. Add the egg and vanilla, and beat until well combined. Drizzle in the half-and-half, and beat at medium-low speed until mostly combined (the mixture will look broken and curdled). Add the flour mixture, and beat just until smooth. Stir in the chopped bacon.

5   Pour the batter evenly into the prepared muffin cups. Moisten your fingers with water, and smooth the surface of the batter in each cup. Using your finger or a small measuring spoon, make a small divot in the center of each, and spoon ¼ teaspoon of the caramel sauce into each divot. Bake until a wooden pick inserted in the center of the scuffin comes out clean, about 15 minutes. Cool in the pan on a wire rack for 5 minutes. Remove the scuffins from the pan, and cool completely on the rack.

6   While the scuffins bake, stir together the clotted cream and remaining 2 tablespoons caramel sauce. Serve the scuffins with the caramel clotted cream.

Before the first season of my cooking show, I was in the Food Network test kitchen, trying to invent a recipe. I had in mind something that was both healthy and decadent. Nearby, several notable chefs were working on their own creations. As an actor with a passion for cooking, I was a trifle insecure, until everybody tasted my dish and gave it rave reviews. A woman I admire said, "Not quite a muffin. But so good." Another chef said, "It tastes like a scone, but kind of like a muffin, too." Suddenly, I lit up. "Oh, it's a scuffin!" And so the scuffin was born. They are so darn cute. As for the ingredients, I love the coconut and cherries for their chewiness, and when I was originally working on this recipe, the yogurt was one of the healthier ingredients. In retrospect, this is not necessarily low in calories, but like many accidental concoctions, that's now beside the point.

Cherry-Coconut Scuffins

SERVES **24**   HANDS-ON **20 MINUTES**   TOTAL **45 MINUTES**

1 Preheat the oven to 350°F. Place baking cups in 2 (24-cup) miniature muffin pans.

2 Combine the flour, baking powder, baking soda, and salt in a medium bowl. Combine the coconut sugar and coconut oil in the bowl of a heavy-duty electric stand mixer fitted with the paddle attachment. Beat at high speed until very light and fluffy, about 4 minutes. Add the eggs, 1 at a time, beating until incorporated after each addition. Add the yogurt and the almond extract; beat at medium-low speed until incorporated. With the mixer running on lowest speed, add the flour mixture, and beat just until the batter comes together (it will resemble cookie dough). Fold in the cherries and ½ cup of the shredded coconut.

3 Place 2 tablespoons of the batter in each prepared muffin cup. Sprinkle evenly with the remaining ¼ cup shredded coconut. Bake until a wooden pick inserted in the center of the scuffin comes out clean and the coconut is toasted on top, about 15 minutes. Cool in the pans on a wire rack for 10 minutes. Remove the scuffins from the pan, and cool completely on the rack.

3 cups all-purpose flour

1 teaspoon baking powder

½ teaspoon baking soda

½ teaspoon table salt

1½ cups unrefined coconut sugar

1 cup coconut oil, at room temperature

2 large eggs

1 cup fat-free plain Greek yogurt

1 teaspoon almond extract

1½ cups dried cherries, coarsely chopped

¾ cup sweetened shredded coconut

EQUIPMENT

You will need 2 (24-cup) miniature muffin pans, or you'll need to bake in two batches. Baking cups are a necessity for this recipe as the batter may stick.

It was spring break, and I wanted to make the kids a special breakfast, but something besides French toast or pancakes—I don't know if they were tired of them, but I was. I went on the Internet in search of ideas and a Dutch Baby caught my eye. A cross between a crepe, a pancake, a soufflé, and a popover, it was not in my repertoire, and I wanted to try it. It turned out beautifully and I impressed even myself. The kids, of course, devoured it. Since then, I came up with my own version. A quick tip: Before you make this, read the recipe all the way through. It's important to know all the steps ahead of time and you have to do them in order. The last step, though, is the best: You get to eat it. Serve it straight from the oven and get ready to fall in love.

Dutch Baby with Lemon Curd

SERVES **4**   HANDS-ON **30 MINUTES**
TOTAL **50 MINUTES PLUS 2 HOURS CHILLING TIME**

1 Make the Lemon Curd: Beat the granulated sugar and butter in a large bowl with an electric mixer at medium speed until fluffy, about 2 minutes. Add the eggs and the egg yolks; beat until combined, about 1 minute. Add the lemon juice; beat until combined, about 1 minute (the mixture will look curdled).

2 Pour the mixture into a medium heavy-bottomed saucepan; cook over low until smooth, about 2 minutes. Increase the heat to medium; cook, stirring constantly, until the mixture coats the back of a spoon, 5 to 7 minutes. (Do not let the mixture come to a boil.) Remove from the heat; stir in the zest. Transfer the mixture to a shallow dish. Place plastic wrap directly on the warm curd (to prevent a film from forming); chill until cold, about 2 hours.

3 Make the Pancake: Place a medium cast-iron skillet in the oven; preheat the oven to 425°F. (Do not remove the skillet while the oven preheats.) Process the flour, milk, eggs, granulated sugar, zest, vanilla, and salt in a blender until smooth and slightly foamy, about 1 minute.

4 Remove the skillet from the oven; melt the butter in the skillet and tilt in all directions to coat the bottom of the skillet. Pour the batter into the skillet; bake until puffed and golden, about 10 minutes. Reduce the temperature to 300°F, and bake until set, about 8 minutes.

5 Remove from the oven. Sprinkle with the powdered sugar. Top with the Lemon Curd and fresh berries. Serve immediately.

| MAKE AHEAD |
The lemon curd can be made in advance and kept up to 5 days in the refrigerator.

⌣ COOKING TIP ⌣
Place your skillet in the oven while you preheat, then add the butter to the pan while the pan is hot—ta-da! A quick trick to melting butter fast.

LEMON CURD

1 cup granulated sugar

6 tablespoons unsalted butter, at room temperature

2 large eggs

2 large egg yolks

⅔ cup fresh lemon juice (from about 6 lemons), plus 1 teaspoon lemon zest

PANCAKE

½ cup all-purpose flour

½ cup whole milk

3 large eggs

1 tablespoon granulated sugar

½ teaspoon lemon zest

½ teaspoon vanilla extract

¼ teaspoon kosher salt

2 tablespoons unsalted butter

ADDITIONAL INGREDIENTS

Powdered sugar

Fresh berries

◆ TRICK TECHNIQUE ◆

You definitely need a cast-iron skillet. Put it in the oven and get it nice and hot while you make the batter. Then pour the batter into the hot skillet, place it back in the oven, and watch it puff up like a soufflé. It deflates when you pull it out, but you'll have the best pancake you've ever tasted.

1 pint fresh or frozen, thawed
   blueberries

1 ripe nectarine, pitted and cut into
   ½-inch pieces

½ teaspoon vanilla extract

3 tablespoons light brown sugar

2 tablespoons lime juice

½ cup plus 2 teaspoons all-purpose
   flour

½ cup uncooked regular rolled oats

½ cup sliced almonds

½ teaspoon ground cardamom

⅛ teaspoon kosher salt

4 tablespoons unsalted butter,
   softened

1 cup low-fat plain Greek yogurt

2 tablespoons honey

1½ teaspoons lime zest

⊶ VARIATION ⊷

The possibilities are endless—substitute
peaches for the nectarines or raspberries
for the blueberries. For a more indulgent
dessert, serve with ice cream or whipped
cream instead of the yogurt.

Probably like you, I go to the grocery store and buy three or four
nectarines, pears, apples, or whatever fruit is in season, and often
find the last one uneaten. When it starts to turn, I shift into efficiency
mode and think, "What can I make?" These are my favorite types of
challenges. This recipe is delicious and a super-easy way to use fruit
that is on the cusp of becoming overripe. It's also an excellent use
for sweet leftovers in the pantry. You can substitute quick-cooking
oats and various nuts for the crumble. I improvise all the time;
experimentation is the road to discovering a new dish you can't
live without. And talk about versatility: The twist of honeyed lime
yogurt convinced me to make this breakfast fare, but it can easily
double as dessert.

Individual Blueberry-Nectarine
Crumbles with Honeyed Lime Yogurt

SERVES **4**   HANDS-ON **15 MINUTES**   TOTAL **55 MINUTES**

1 Preheat the oven to 375°F. Gently toss together the blueberries, nectarine,
   vanilla, 2 tablespoons of the brown sugar, 1 tablespoon of the lime juice,
   and 2 teaspoons of the flour in a medium bowl. Divide evenly among
   4 (8-ounce) ramekins.

2 Combine the oats, almonds, cardamom, salt, and remaining ½ cup flour
   and 1 tablespoon brown sugar in a medium bowl. Add the butter. Using
   your fingers, blend until fully incorporated. Break the mixture into
   small clumps, and divide evenly among the ramekins to cover the
   blueberry mixture.

3 Place the ramekins on a rimmed baking sheet. Bake until the filling
   is bubbly and the topping is golden, about 30 minutes. Let stand for
   10 minutes.

4 Stir together the yogurt, honey, lime zest, and remaining 1 tablespoon lime
   juice in a small bowl. Top the warm crumbles with the yogurt mixture.

Learning how to make rugelach was a secret desire of mine for years. I bought them in my local grocery store and loved them. They tasted like cookies, and occasionally I ate them for breakfast. They were a perfect grab-and-go starter with my coffee, which is why they fell in this chapter. I never thought I could learn how to make them, but through practice I developed this recipe. One leisurely morning, as my husband, Tom, and I were enjoying them with our coffee on the patio, I looked up from my crossword puzzle and said, "Oh my God, I can make rugelach." You can, too. It's not hard. Pay attention to the way the cream cheese dough pairs with the chocolate and nuts—that taste is memorable. The sweetness and tartness and the way the chocolate melts and the bottom crisps up— you are going to make these all the time.

Chocolate Walnut Rugelach

MAKES **32**   HANDS-ON **35 MINUTES**   TOTAL **3 HOURS, 45 MINUTES**

1 cup all-purpose flour, plus more for work surface

3 tablespoons granulated sugar

½ teaspoon kosher salt

½ cup cold unsalted butter, cut into cubes

½ cup cold cream cheese, cut into cubes

½ cup apricot jam

½ cup chopped walnuts

¼ cup packed light brown sugar

½ teaspoon ground cinnamon

½ cup miniature semisweet chocolate chips

1 large egg, lightly beaten

1 Combine 1 cup of the flour, 1 tablespoon of the granulated sugar, and ¼ teaspoon of the salt in a food processor; pulse to combine, 10 to 12 times. Add the butter and cream cheese; pulse until the dough begins to form small clumps, about 16 times. Divide the dough in half; shape each half into a flat disk. Wrap with plastic wrap, and chill for 2 hours.

2 Preheat the oven to 350°F. Process the apricot jam in the food processor until smooth, about 15 seconds. Transfer to a small bowl. Add the walnuts, brown sugar, cinnamon, and remaining ¼ teaspoon salt to the processor; process until the nuts are finely chopped, about 10 seconds.

3 Unwrap 1 dough disk, and roll into an 11-inch circle on a lightly floured surface. Spread ¼ cup of the jam evenly over the dough; sprinkle evenly with half of the walnut mixture (about ½ cup) and ¼ cup of the chocolate chips. Press the filling gently into the dough. Use a pizza cutter or sharp knife to cut the dough round into 16 wedges. Roll up each wedge, beginning with the wide end and ending with the point. Place the rugelach, point sides down, on a baking sheet lined with parchment paper. Repeat with the remaining dough round, apricot jam, walnut mixture, and chocolate chips. Freeze for 15 minutes.

4 Brush the rugelach with the beaten egg; sprinkle with the remaining 2 tablespoons granulated sugar. Bake until deep golden brown, 20 to 25 minutes. Cool on the baking sheets on wire racks about 10 minutes; remove the rugelach from the baking sheets to the wire racks, and cool completely, about 20 minutes.

½ cup Neufchâtel cheese, softened

1 tablespoon Sriracha chili sauce

2 teaspoons honey

1 everything bagel, split

2 tablespoons salted butter

2 large eggs

⅛ teaspoon kosher salt

⅛ teaspoon black pepper

1 teaspoon chopped chives

I like a hearty breakfast with great flavors. Some days my body craves a substantial meal in the morning, and this is a simple, straightforward way to satisfy that need. I used to cut a hole in a slice of toast and fry an egg in the middle for my son when he was a little boy. He loved them. Bagels already have the hole in the middle so it's even easier—and I love that. This is a typical bagel and egg until you add the Sriracha sauce, a hot sauce made from peppers, garlic, vinegar, salt, and sugar. For some reason, it goes with everything, and especially this dish. The cheese and honey mixed together, then splashed with Sriracha deliver a morning oomph that makes this seemingly ordinary dish quite extraordinary.

Egg-in-a-Bagel-Hole

SERVES **2**   HANDS-ON **15 MINUTES**   TOTAL **15 MINUTES**

1 Beat the cheese, Sriracha, and honey in a medium bowl with an electric mixer at high speed until light and fluffy, about 1 minute. Set aside.

2 Using a 2½-inch round cutter, cut out the center of the bagel to create a larger hole.

3 Melt the butter in a large nonstick skillet over medium. Add the bagel halves, cut sides down; cook until very lightly browned, about 1 minute. Turn the bagel halves, and break 1 egg into each bagel hole. Cover and cook until the bagel is browned, the egg whites are set, and the yolks are runny, 3 to 5 minutes. Transfer to a plate.

4 Sprinkle the eggs evenly with the salt and pepper and the chopped chives; spread the bagel halves evenly with the whipped cheese mixture. Serve immediately.

3 cups all-purpose baking mix

1 pound ground spicy pork sausage

4 cups shredded sharp Cheddar cheese
   (about 16 ounces)

1 tablespoon pure maple syrup, plus
   more for serving

1 tablespoon hot sauce, plus more
   for serving

2 teaspoons olive oil

8 large eggs

½ teaspoon kosher salt

½ teaspoon black pepper

8 pepper Jack cheese slices

8 bacon slices, cooked

MAKE AHEAD

Make this the night before to grab on-the-go in the morning.

VARIATION

You can use different cheeses. Instead of pepper Jack, for instance, try Cheddar or regular Jack cheese. And if you think the biscuit has enough flavor, you can skip the bacon and cheese and just top with an egg and not sacrifice any flavor. Whatever you desire.

Some tastes stay with you for your entire life, and for me, this dish is one of them. When I was a teenager, my mom taught me how to make sausage and cheese bites, and I have savored their rich, comforting taste since taking my first batch out of the oven. It's one of those old recipes from the 1950s. She made them for my dad's poker games, and always made sure there were leftovers that I ate for breakfast. Now, jump ahead 30-plus years after I last refreshed drinks for my dad's poker buddies and I had those sausage and cheese bites on my mind. They were basically biscuits, as I recalled, and I thought they would make a delicious breakfast sandwich if I simply put an egg in the middle with a little bit of bacon and some more spicy cheese. I tried it, and they were super good. In my mind, I simply built on a classic. Friends say they're perfect for a hearty breakfast or a hangover.

Breakfast Biscuit Sammies

SERVES **8**   HANDS-ON **30 MINUTES**   TOTAL **1 HOUR, 15 MINUTES**

1 Preheat the oven to 400°F. Combine the baking mix, sausage, cheese, syrup, and hot sauce in a large bowl. Shape into 16 (1¼-inch) balls and, with wet hands, flatten each slightly into a disk. Place the disks about 1 inch apart on a parchment paper-lined baking sheet. Bake until golden and cooked through, about 15 minutes. Cool completely, about 30 minutes.

2 Heat the olive oil in a large nonstick skillet over medium-high. Add the eggs, reduce the heat to medium-low, cover, and cook until the whites are set and the yolks are soft, about 2 minutes, or to the desired degree of doneness. Sprinkle with ¼ teaspoon each of the salt and pepper.

3 Place 1 slice of the cheese on the bottom half of each sausage biscuit. Top with the eggs and bacon. Top with the remaining sausage biscuit halves. Serve with more hot sauce or maple syrup, if desired.

I love arugula. I adore the spicy, peppery taste of this hearty green leaf and constantly try to find new ways to use it. It's always in my fridge. As a result, this recipe has become a staple. Don't let the word frittata scare you. It's basically a baked egg dish—a quiche without the crust. Besides arugula, I always have goat cheese, feta, or Parmesan in the fridge. We have tomatoes from the garden, and the rest is simple. This is my go-to when I want a substantial breakfast but also know I need to eat light and healthy, like before a hike, a morning photo shoot, or before we set off on a long weekend road trip. It's an excellent choice and goes well with fresh melon or a side of mixed fruit. It also looks beautiful on the plate.

Egg White Frittata with Arugula, Tomato, and Goat Cheese

SERVES **4**   HANDS-ON **20 MINUTES**   TOTAL **30 MINUTES**

1 Preheat the oven to 400°F. Heat the oil in a 10-inch nonstick ovenproof skillet over medium. Add the onion, and cook, stirring often, until tender and slightly caramelized, about 10 minutes. Add the arugula, and cook, stirring constantly, until wilted, 1 to 2 minutes. Reduce the heat to medium-low.

2 Beat the egg whites and mustard in a medium bowl with an electric mixer at high speed until foamy.

3 Return the heat to medium, and pour the egg white mixture into the skillet. Cook until the bottom is set, lifting the sides occasionally to allow the raw egg white to drip to the bottom of the skillet, about 3 minutes. Top with the tomato slices, and sprinkle with the salt and pepper. Top evenly with the goat cheese.

4 Transfer the skillet to the oven, and bake until the eggs are set, about 8 minutes. Drizzle with the balsamic glaze, sprinkle with the basil, if desired, and serve immediately.

2 tablespoons olive oil

½ cup thinly sliced sweet onion

4 cups loosely packed baby arugula

8 large egg whites

2 teaspoons Dijon mustard

1 medium plum tomato, thinly sliced crosswise

½ teaspoon kosher salt

¼ teaspoon black pepper

½ cup crumbled goat cheese

1 tablespoon balsamic glaze

Handful of baby basil leaves (optional)

◁ VARIATION ▷

Don't have arugula and goat cheese on hand? Substitute spinach and feta.

EQUIPMENT

You will need a nonstick ovenproof skillet for this dish.

6 turkey bacon slices

8 large eggs

2 tablespoons water

½ teaspoon kosher salt

¼ teaspoon black pepper

2 tablespoons olive oil

1 cup cherry tomatoes

4 ounces sliced cremini mushrooms

1 cup chopped zucchini

1 garlic clove, minced

2 tablespoons chopped fresh flat-leaf
  parsley, plus more for serving

MAKE AHEAD

Make the filling the night before for
quicker omelets in the morning.

I grew up a cereal girl. Eggs were for the weekends. I've changed, as you can tell, but this all-in omelet is a favorite of mine for weekend mornings when Tom and I wake up super hungry or feel like brunch. I also like that I can empty the fridge into this omelet. When my veggies have only a day or two left, they go into this dish. Sometimes I chop them the night before and get my prep done, making this even quicker in the morning so I get more time with my crossword puzzle. Omelets need attention as they cook; it's all about pulling the edges off the side of the pan and making sure the egg cooks without overcooking. I build my omelet slowly and then spread the ingredients evenly. If you want to fancy it up, serve with a few avocado slices on the side. This dish is a winner, and you'll feel like one, too.

All-in Omelets with Turkey Bacon

SERVES **4**   HANDS-ON **20 MINUTES**   TOTAL **45 MINUTES**

1 Preheat the oven to 400°F. Place the turkey bacon in a single layer on an aluminum foil-lined rimmed baking sheet. Bake until crispy, about 15 minutes. Cool for 10 minutes; crumble and set aside.

2 Whisk together the eggs, water, salt, and pepper in a bowl. Set aside.

3 Heat 1 tablespoon of the oil in a large nonstick skillet over medium-high. Add the tomatoes and mushrooms; cook, stirring occasionally, until the tomatoes have burst and the mushrooms are browned, about 8 minutes. Add the zucchini and garlic; cook, stirring often, until tender, about 4 minutes. Transfer the mixture to a bowl. Fold in the crumbled bacon and parsley. Wipe the skillet clean.

4 Heat 1½ teaspoons of the oil in the skillet over medium-high. Add half of the egg mixture, tilting the skillet to spread evenly. Cook until the edges begin to set, about 1 minute. Using a rubber spatula, lift the edges of the omelet while tilting the skillet to allow the uncooked egg mixture to drip to the bottom of the skillet. Cook just until the center is set, about 1 minute. Sprinkle half of the tomato mixture over the omelet. Run the spatula around the edges of the omelet to loosen it from the skillet; fold the omelet in half to cover the filling. Transfer the omelet to a plate; cover loosely with foil to keep warm. Repeat the process with the remaining oil, egg mixture, and tomato mixture.

5 Sprinkle the omelets with some parsley; serve immediately.

GETTING THROUGH THE DAY

Lunch doesn't have to be lunch—at least as I've always known it. I had this revelation one day after I returned home from a morning of meetings and errands. I dropped my stuff on the dining room table, kicked off my shoes, and went into the kitchen. I was hungry, but I didn't know for what—lunch, a snack, something between lunch and a snack.

What I wanted was the type of lunch I had while on vacation: a thoughtful dish with simple but distinct flavors that would touch my tongue and filter straight into my brain where the response would be a grateful, "Thank you, this is perfect. Let's relax and enjoy."

Fifteen minutes later, I was eating an avocado open-face sandwich outside on the patio. I put a slice of lemon in my water and picked some flowers for the table. This delightful respite forever changed my attitude about lunch. From then on, I quit thinking about it as the dutiful meal I ate between twelve and one o'clock, as if I were still in grade school, hurrying to finish my peanut butter and jelly or bologna sandwich before the bell rang.

Instead, I approach this time, whenever it occurs, as a chance to recharge, as if I were on vacation. Whether my break is 30 minutes or three hours, I treat myself to a nice meal. Even if I fix myself a sandwich, I use only fresh, seasonal ingredients. I plate my food on nice china. I try to be creative. At the end, I find I am more than full. I am fulfilled—and I get through the day feeling refreshed and satisfied.

In this chapter, I selected recipes that have that same effect on me. They are simple but delicious and filled with strong, refreshing flavors that can transform a weekend afternoon into a celebration. Fresh green apples, buttery avocado, quinoa, chunks of Maine lobster, bacon, tuna, cheeses, and my beloved arugula. These are the ingredients you'll find. They are chockfull of taste and texture.

Of course, you can make these dishes for just yourself, as I frequently do, but they are best when shared, and that notion also entered into my selection process. I pictured people coming to your house for a midday meal. I considered how busy all of us are these days. I thought about the different types of issues everyone puts aside as they sit at the table. Whether your guests are family or friends, I wanted them to stop after their first bite, look at you, and acknowledge their day just changed for the better.

Every day is different, and your middle of the day meal can and should reflect that, too. It can be anything you want. It can, and should, get you through the day. Go for it!

Doesn't it seem like every cook and their mother has a recipe for avocado toast? And there's a reason why . . . it's so damn good. I used to be afraid of the fat in avocado, but I learned it's the kind of fat our bodies need. Once I got the clearance, I started making avocado toast all of the time, but I do it with a twist. Adding ricotta provides a nice creamy texture, which I balance out with the salt from the capers and the crunch from the sunflower seeds, which are a good source of vitamin E. The other thing I love about this open-face avocado sammie is the pretty factor. It looks so pretty on a plate, and because it tastes so fresh and clean, it makes you feel pretty, too. Huge bonus.

Avocado Open-Face Sandwiches

SERVES **6**   HANDS-ON **15 MINUTES**   TOTAL **25 MINUTES**

1   Prepare the Ricotta Mixture: Stir together all the ingredients in a bowl. Set aside until ready to use.

2   Prepare the Open-Face Sandwiches: Place the shallot slices in a small bowl with ice water to cover. Let stand for 10 minutes. Drain.

3   Using your fingers, stir together the sea salt and lemon zest in a bowl.

4   Top each toasted bread slice with about 2 tablespoons of the Ricotta Mixture. Top each with 2 avocado slices, 2 tomato slices, 2 teaspoons shallot slices, and 1 teaspoon sunflower seeds. Sprinkle each with ⅛ teaspoon of the lemon salt. Cut the sandwiches in half diagonally, and serve immediately.

RICOTTA MIXTURE

¾ cup whole-milk ricotta, drained

1 tablespoon capers, drained, rinsed, and crushed

1 tablespoon extra-virgin olive oil

½ tablespoon lemon zest, plus 1 tablespoon fresh lemon juice

¼ teaspoon kosher salt

¼ teaspoon black pepper

OPEN-FACE SANDWICHES

1 small shallot, sliced

2 tablespoons flaked sea salt

1 tablespoon lemon zest

6 sourdough bread slices, toasted

1 ripe avocado, cut into 12 slices

2 heirloom tomatoes, each cut into 6 slices

2 tablespoons salted sunflower seeds

⚘ COOKING TIP ⚘

You'll have extra lemon salt, which I like to use on everything from steamed or roasted broccoli or asparagus to sautéed mushrooms or grilled shrimp.

MAKE AHEAD

Make the ricotta mixture the night before to let the flavors develop.

¼ cup dill pickle relish

2 tablespoons whole-grain mustard

1 tablespoon thinly sliced fresh chives

1 teaspoon honey

1 apple (such as Gala or Pink Lady),
  sliced into half-moons

1 tablespoon fresh lemon juice

12 Hawaiian sweet rolls, split

12 sharp Cheddar cheese slices

8 ounces thinly sliced Black Forest ham

1½ cups loosely packed baby arugula

◆ TRICK TECHNIQUE ◆

I have an ingenious shortcut: I take a big
bread knife, hold down the whole package
of rolls, cut all 12 across the center, open
it up like it's this big square sandwich,
and lay down all the meat, cheese and
relish. Top off with the other half, then
cut each one individually. It makes your
life super easy.

Finger foods. There's something about eating with your hands that makes food taste better—especially sliders, and especially sliders that combine salty cheese, ham, and crisp apple or pear. I put this favorite combo of mine between sweet, doughy Hawaiian rolls and fell instantly and deeply in love. You feel like you're getting a whole sandwich when in reality the portion size is halved. But the taste is concentrated and even more delicious. Plus, they're cute, easy, and fun, which makes them perfect for a party.

Ham, Apple, and Cheddar Sliders

SERVES **12**   HANDS-ON **20 MINUTES**   TOTAL **20 MINUTES**

Stir together the relish, mustard, chives, and honey in a small bowl. Toss the apple slices with the lemon juice. Spread the relish mixture on the cut sides of the rolls. Build the sandwiches with the cheese, apple slices, ham, and arugula.

SAUSAGE AND
PEPPERS SLIDERS
PG 52

2 tablespoons olive oil

1 red or orange bell pepper, sliced

1 large shallot, sliced

1 garlic clove, sliced

8 ounces tomato sauce

1¼ pounds Italian sausage (sweet, hot, or a mix), casings removed

8 slider buns or small potato rolls, split and lightly toasted

2 tablespoons roughly chopped fresh flat-leaf parsley

A while ago Tom told me that one of his favorite dishes is sausage and peppers. Naturally, I wanted to come up with a sausage and peppers dish, but how much can you do there? I mean, sausage and peppers is sausage and peppers. So like the true Italian that I am, I stuck 'em between two slices of bread and called it a day. I didn't actually call it a day. Instead, I called out to Tom and the kids that dinner was ready, and ever since, these sliders have become one of those dishes that I make over and over again. They're simple, satisfying, and they combine my favorite flavors—sweet and spicy—so you get both and don't have to choose!

Sausage and Peppers Sliders
SERVES **8**   HANDS-ON **30 MINUTES**   TOTAL **30 MINUTES**

1 Heat 1 tablespoon of the oil in a medium skillet over medium. Add the bell pepper, shallot, and garlic, and cook, stirring occasionally, until soft, 10 to 12 minutes. Stir in the tomato sauce, and cook until slightly thickened, about 3 minutes.

2 Form the sausage into 8 (½-inch-thick) patties. Heat the remaining 1 tablespoon oil in a large nonstick skillet over medium-high. Add the sausage patties, and cook until golden brown on both sides and cooked through, about 4 minutes per side.

3 Place the sausage patties on the bottom halves of the buns. Top evenly with the pepper mixture; sprinkle with the parsley. Cover with the top halves of the buns, and serve immediately.

BEEF

4 pounds boneless chuck roast, trimmed and quartered

1 (14½-ounce) can diced tomatoes with basil and oregano, drained

2 red, orange, or yellow bell peppers, sliced

1 small yellow onion, halved and thinly sliced

2 garlic cloves, chopped

2 teaspoons Italian Seasoning (recipe follows)

½ teaspoon fennel seeds

2½ teaspoons kosher salt

1 teaspoon black pepper

AÏOLI

1 large pasteurized egg

2 garlic cloves, finely grated

1 teaspoon Dijon mustard

½ cup extra-virgin olive oil

½ cup vegetable oil

1 (16-ounce) jar giardiniera, drained

¼ teaspoon kosher salt

¼ teaspoon black pepper

ADDITIONAL INGREDIENT

4 (12- to 14-inch-long) French bread loaves; halved lengthwise, split, and lightly toasted

The funny thing about this sandwich is it's a lot harder to say the name than it is to assemble. You'd be surprised how easy it is to make aïoli. The food processor does all the work, and then the rest of this sandwich is what I like to call good messy. You get the acid, saltiness, and tartness from the giardiniera and then combine it with the beef . . . amazeballs. It's hearty, juicy, savory, decadent, and perfect for a tailgating party, or just a Sunday or Monday get-together. I grew up with three brothers, so I always want to feed people a hearty meal. I also love using my slow cooker, and this sandwich puts it to great use.

Slow-Cooker Beef Sandwiches with Giardiniera Aïoli

SERVES **8**   HANDS-ON **15 MINUTES**   TOTAL **8 HOURS, 15 MINUTES**

1 Make the Beef: Combine the chuck roast, tomatoes, bell peppers, onion, garlic, Italian Seasoning, fennel seeds, salt, and black pepper in a slow cooker. Cover and cook on LOW until the meat is cooked through and shreds easily with a fork, about 8 hours.

2 Skim and discard the fat from the surface. Remove the chuck roast, and coarsely shred with 2 forks. Toss the meat with ¼ cup of the cooking liquid.

3 Make the Aïoli: Process the egg, garlic, and mustard in a food processor until combined. With the food processor running, slowly pour in the olive oil and vegetable oil in a very slow, steady stream through the food chute until fully incorporated. Add the giardiniera, and pulse until finely chopped and incorporated. Stir in the salt and black pepper.

4 Spread about 2 tablespoons of the aïoli on the cut side of each piece of the bread. Assemble the sandwiches with the shredded beef. Serve immediately.

MAKE AHEAD

You can make the aïoli up to 3 days ahead and store it in the fridge.

MOM'S ONION RINGS
PG 206

Italian Seasoning

MAKES ABOUT ⅔ **CUP**   HANDS-ON **5 MINUTES**   TOTAL **5 MINUTES**

Stir together all the ingredients. Store in a jar with a tight-fitting lid in a cool dark place for up to a year.

☞ COOKING TIP ☜

Not only is it fun to experiment making your own seasoning, but it's money-saving, too.

ITALIAN SEASONING

3 tablespoons dried basil

3 tablespoons dried marjoram

3 tablespoons dried oregano

3 tablespoons dried parsley

1 tablespoon granulated garlic

1 teaspoon dried rosemary

1 teaspoon dried thyme

¼ teaspoon crushed red pepper

3 (7-ounce) fresh or frozen, thawed lobster tails

8 bacon slices

1 small shallot, finely chopped

1 tablespoon capers, drained and chopped

1 teaspoon lemon zest, plus 1 tablespoon fresh lemon juice

⅓ cup plus 2 tablespoons mayonnaise

½ teaspoon kosher salt

¼ teaspoon black pepper

8 white bread slices, toasted

2 medium tomatoes, sliced

4 green leaf lettuce leaves, torn in half

┌─────────────────┐
│ MAKE AHEAD   │
└─────────────────┘

You can make the lobster salad up to 3 days ahead; store in an airtight container in the fridge.

◆ TRICK TECHNIQUE ◆

Your cooking shears are your best friend when it comes to preparing this salad. Just cut the lobster shells, pull out the meat, and snip it into pieces. See page 26 for another trick—baking your bacon!

The first time I ever touched upon this hybrid heaven was when I made these for my good old Louisiana girlfriend, Faith Ford. Faith is one of my favorite people to cook for because she loves and appreciates food. But let's be honest, who wouldn't love and appreciate a creamy lobster roll fused with a crunchy, salty BLT? This sandwich is decadence at its best, which also means it can get pricey and labor-intensive. Here's my time- and wallet-friendly tip: Buy a frozen lobster tail as opposed to buying a whole lobster. It's a lot easier, and by a lot I mean . . . when there's lobster salad, juicy tomato and crispy bacon on the other side, time is of the essence.

Lobster BLTs

SERVES **4** HANDS-ON **20 MINUTES** TOTAL **35 MINUTES**

1 Bring a medium stockpot of water to a boil over high. Add the lobster tails, and boil until the shells are bright red and the lobster is just cooked through, about 7 minutes. Drain and rinse with cold water. Let stand until cool enough to handle. Remove the meat from the shells; coarsely chop.

2 Place the bacon in a large skillet. Cook over medium, turning occasionally, until crisp and browned, 10 to 12 minutes. Transfer the bacon to a plate lined with paper towels.

3 Stir together the shallot, capers, lemon zest, lemon juice, and ⅓ cup of the mayonnaise in a medium bowl. Add the chopped lobster, salt, and pepper, and stir to combine.

4 Spread each of 4 toasted bread slices with a scant ¼ cup of the lobster salad and top each with 2 bacon slices. Add 2 tomato slices and 2 pieces lettuce. Spread the remaining 2 tablespoons mayonnaise evenly on the remaining 4 bread slices. Cover the sandwiches with bread slices, and serve immediately.

A serious misconception is that the good ol' days of enjoying comfort food are dead and done, like an oil-soaked empty pizza box sitting at the bottom of the trashcan. People, this just isn't true. Hearty, warm comfort food can be healthy and nutritious. Tuna melts are one of my favorite examples. Tuna, of course, is rich in iron and protein. And tuna salad is so easy to make. When I first lived by myself, I made open-face tuna salad sandwiches all of the time. To this day, I find the sight of bubbling cheese very beautiful. But these days I'm less concerned with a small hill of cheese than I am with making sure my food has nutritious value. Whenever I make this for lunch, I add avocado and a bitter green, like arugula. A crunchier lettuce pairs well, too. Sometimes I do it with romaine leaves, thinly sliced red onion, and a pickle or two. And maybe a handful of potato chips on the side.

Tuna Melts

SERVES **4**   HANDS-ON **30 MINUTES**   TOTAL **30 MINUTES**

1 Place the tuna, celery, egg, mayonnaise, capers, parsley, lemon zest, lemon juice, salt, and pepper in a medium bowl. Stir gently to blend, breaking the tuna into smaller pieces.

2 Place the bread slices on a flat work surface; top each of 4 slices with 1 cheese slice. Spoon about ½ cup of the tuna mixture over the cheese on each, and top evenly with the avocado, tomato, arugula, and remaining cheese. Cover with the remaining bread slices. Lightly brush the outsides of each sandwich with olive oil.

3 Heat a large nonstick skillet or griddle over medium-high until hot. Place the sandwiches, in batches if necessary, in the hot skillet, and cook until the cheese is melted and the bread is golden brown and crispy, about 2 minutes per side. Cut the sandwiches in half, and serve immediately.

4 (2.6-ounce) pouches solid white albacore tuna in water

4 celery stalks with leaves, chopped (about 1 cup)

1 hard-cooked egg, chopped

½ cup mayonnaise

¼ cup drained capers or chopped pimiento-stuffed Spanish olives

2 tablespoons chopped fresh flat-leaf parsley

½ teaspoon lemon zest, plus 1 tablespoon fresh lemon juice

½ teaspoon kosher salt

¼ teaspoon black pepper

8 hearty white deli bread slices

8 Havarti cheese slices

1 ripe avocado, quartered and sliced

1 large tomato, sliced

1 cup loosely packed arugula

Olive oil

INGREDIENT NOTE
Solid white albacore tuna has a clean, not fishy, taste and allows other ingredients to shine.

⊱ VARIATION ⊰

There's tons of room for variation with this sandwich, particularly with the choice of tuna. Consider your preference before cooking. I prefer jarred Italian tuna to the canned albacore tuna. The jarred tuna comes in oil, so I use less mayo later on.

1 tablespoon olive oil

1½ cups diced sweet onion (about 2 onions)

3 garlic cloves, minced

1 cup Italian-seasoned breadcrumbs

¼ cup whole milk

2 tablespoons chopped fresh flat-leaf parsley

1 tablespoon Worcestershire sauce

1½ teaspoons kosher salt

½ teaspoon black pepper

1 large egg, lightly beaten

½ cup ketchup

1 pound ground turkey

1 pound ground sweet turkey Italian sausage (casings removed if not using bulk)

2 tablespoons mayonnaise

1 tablespoon light brown sugar

1 tablespoon Sriracha chili sauce

10 provolone cheese slices

10 ciabatta rolls, split

10 cooked bacon slices, halved

Dill pickle chips

⚑ VARIATION ⚑

You can use hot Italian sausage instead of sweet to amp up the heat.

I used to make meatloaf for my son, Wolfie, every Thursday night. While he was doing his homework, I could stand within eyesight of him because it took me awhile to mix and make the ingredients. It was a good routine, at least in my mind it was. I remember wanting to make a great burger that was healthier than a traditional ground beef burger, and on one of those Thursday nights while I was making my turkey meatloaf, I had an epiphany: *I love my meatloaf, why not just make a turkey meatloaf burger?*

Turkey Meatloaf Burgers

SERVES **10**   HANDS-ON **30 MINUTES**   TOTAL **30 MINUTES**

1 Heat the olive oil in a medium skillet over medium-high. Add the onion and garlic, and cook, stirring often, until the onion is softened and very lightly browned, about 6 minutes. Remove from the heat, and cool slightly.

2 Stir together the breadcrumbs, milk, parsley, Worcestershire, salt, pepper, egg, and ¼ cup of the ketchup in a large bowl. Add the ground meat, and gently combine using your hands. Let the mixture stand for 5 minutes.

3 Preheat the grill to medium (350°F to 450°F). Shape the meat mixture into 10 (about ¼-pound) patties. Using your finger, make a slight indentation into the middle of each patty. (This helps to allow for plumping while the patty cooks on the grill.)

4 Stir together the mayonnaise, brown sugar, Sriracha, and remaining ¼ cup ketchup in a small bowl.

5 Place the patties on oiled grates; grill, covered, until they are no longer pink in the center, 4 to 5 minutes per side, arranging 1 slice of cheese on top of each patty during the last few minutes of grilling. Serve the patties in the ciabatta rolls each topped with 2 bacon halves, pickles, and dollops of the Sriracha mixture. Serve immediately.

BABY GREENS SALAD WITH
PICKLED RED ONIONS AND
CHAMPAGNE VINAIGRETTE
PG 64

Pickling is so damn easy. I had no idea until I tried it one day. Anyone can pickle. Just put together the pickle mixture in a bowl or a jar, add your veggies or whatever you're going to pickle, and then let it sit in the fridge. It's that easy, which is why I always have pickled red onions in my fridge. They add a nice tart bite to salads, burgers, sandwiches . . . everything, really. Yummy.

Baby Greens Salad with Pickled Red Onions and Champagne Vinaigrette

SERVES **4**   HANDS-ON **10 MINUTES**   TOTAL **30 MINUTES**

1 Make the Salad: Bring the white vinegar, water, sugar, and salt to a simmer in a small saucepan over medium-high. Add the onion, and return to a simmer. Remove from the heat; let stand for 15 minutes. Drain.

2 Place the greens in a large bowl; add the tomatoes and 2 tablespoons of the pickled onions. Store the remaining pickled onions in the refrigerator. Toss to combine.

3 Make the Vinaigrette: Combine all the ingredients in a jar. Cover with a lid, and shake vigorously until fully combined.

4 Add just enough Vinaigrette to lightly coat the salad, and toss well to coat. Add additional salt and pepper, if desired. Store any remaining vinaigrette in an airtight container in the refrigerator for up to 1 week.

SALAD

½ cup distilled white vinegar

½ cup water

2 tablespoons granulated sugar

1 teaspoon kosher salt

1 medium red onion, thinly sliced

5 ounces baby greens

1 cup cherry tomatoes, halved (about 6 ounces)

VINAIGRETTE

½ cup extra-virgin olive oil

3 tablespoons Champagne vinegar

1 teaspoon honey

1 teaspoon Dijon mustard

½ teaspoon kosher salt

⅛ teaspoon black pepper

| MAKE AHEAD |

The pickled onions can be made up to 2 weeks ahead. Store in an airtight container.

⚬ VARIATION ⚬

Add some grilled chicken or shrimp to turn this into a light dinner.

I love this salad either on its own for a light summer dinner, or as a side dish to the Turkey Meatloaf Burgers (page 62). I like to finely chop my lettuce because I always eat my salads right away (your chopped lettuce may brown if you don't eat it right away). Let's talk about the dressing for a minute. It can be made ahead of time, and it can also be used as a dip for crudités. Don't be afraid of the anchovy in it. Here's the thing about anchovies in dressings—they don't add a fishy flavor, they increase the saltiness. Iodized or salt flakes just don't cut it. Anchovies are really the best way to get a more intense and well-rounded salt flavor in your dressing.

Avocado and Grilled Corn Salad with Green Goddess Dressing

SERVES **4**   HANDS-ON **25 MINUTES**   TOTAL **25 MINUTES**

1 Preheat the grill to medium-high (about 450°F). Rub the corn and jalapeño with the oil. Grill, uncovered, turning occasionally, until tender and charred in spots, about 6 minutes for the jalapeño and 12 minutes for the corn. Let stand until cool enough to handle. Cut the kernels from the cobs, and place the kernels in a large bowl. Add the romaine and avocado to the bowl.

2 Remove the stem and seeds from the jalapeño. Process the jalapeño, mayonnaise, buttermilk, parsley, chives, lemon juice, dill, anchovy, garlic, and salt in a blender until smooth.

3 Add just enough of the dressing to coat the salad; toss to coat. Store the remaining dressing in an airtight container in the refrigerator for up to 1 week.

3 ears fresh corn, husks removed

1 small jalapeño chile

1 tablespoon vegetable oil

1 romaine lettuce heart, chopped

1 large, ripe avocado, chopped

¾ cup mayonnaise

⅓ cup buttermilk

¼ cup chopped fresh flat-leaf parsley

3 tablespoons chopped fresh chives

1½ tablespoons fresh lemon juice

1 tablespoon chopped fresh dill

1 anchovy fillet

1 small garlic clove, grated

½ teaspoon kosher salt

AVOCADO AND GRILLED
CORN SALAD WITH GREEN
GODDESS DRESSING
PG 65

FENNEL SALAD WITH GOAT
CHEESE AND PINE NUTS
PG 68

3 tablespoons extra-virgin olive oil

1 tablespoon red wine vinegar

½ teaspoon kosher salt

½ teaspoon black pepper

3 cups loosely packed baby arugula leaves (about 2½ ounces)

1 fennel bulb, fronds chopped, bulb thinly sliced using a mandoline

½ cup crumbled goat cheese

2 tablespoons pine nuts, toasted

MAKE AHEAD

The vinaigrette can be made up to a week ahead and stored in an airtight container in the fridge.

VARIATION

Don't like goat cheese? You can use feta instead, and any other toasted nut of your choice.

This is my favorite salad because I love fennel. For whatever reason, I don't like black licorice, but I love fennel . . . yeah, I can't figure it out either! Anyway, I remember the first time I ever ate fennel: My Sicilian friends were over cooking dinner and they threw the fennel on the grill. I asked, "What are you doing? What is that?" My friends said they ate it all the time in Italy. I tried it, and that was it. Done. Fennel is now one of my favorite ingredients. You can roast it, grill it, slice it thinly, use it as crudité . . . it's versatile and has so much flavor. I love how the creamy goat cheese and crunch from the pine nuts offset the bitterness in this salad. It's the perfect combination of flavors.

Fennel Salad with Goat Cheese and Pine Nuts

SERVES **2**   HANDS-ON **20 MINUTES**   TOTAL **20 MINUTES**

Whisk together the oil, vinegar, salt, and pepper in a small bowl. Combine the arugula and the fennel bulb slices in a medium bowl. Drizzle with the vinaigrette, and toss to coat. Top with the chopped fennel fronds, crumbled goat cheese, and toasted pine nuts.

Bacon is a great gateway to salads. In my experience, add bacon to any salad and it's infinitely more appetizing. This salad, for example, was a recipe we did for a grilling episode of the show. I wasn't excited about the strawberries (because I'm not a big fan) and Tom, Wolfie, and my brother Patrick weren't enthused about the salad. But when you combine strawberries with a tangy dressing and warm, crisp bacon, it simply works. If only we had taken before and after pictures that day. Skeptical faces morphed into very pleased, well-fed chins. I mean faces. This salad is also a great dish to bring to a potluck. For a good summer dinner, I like pairing this with my burgers, and if Wolfie's around, I'll make sweet potato fries, too, because he loves those.

Spinach and Strawberry Salad with Warm Bacon Vinaigrette

SERVES **4**   HANDS-ON **15 MINUTES**   TOTAL **15 MINUTES**

1 Place the bacon in a skillet. Cook over medium, stirring occasionally, until browned and crisp, about 10 minutes. Transfer the bacon to a plate lined with paper towels, reserving 1 tablespoon of the drippings in the skillet. Add the sugar and mustard to the skillet, and stir until the sugar dissolves. Whisk in the vinegar, oil, salt, and pepper.

2 Combine the spinach, strawberries, shallot, and bacon in a bowl. Pour the bacon vinaigrette over the salad; toss to coat. Serve immediately.

4 to 6 bacon slices, chopped

1¼ teaspoons granulated sugar

1 teaspoon whole-grain mustard

2 tablespoons red wine vinegar

1 tablespoon olive oil

¼ teaspoon kosher salt

¼ teaspoon black pepper

6 ounces baby spinach

1½ cups sliced fresh strawberries (about 7 ounces)

1 medium shallot, thinly sliced

⚬ COOKING TIP ⚬

This is when I like to fry up my bacon because I'm using the bacon drippings for my warm dressing.

¾ cup uncooked quinoa, thoroughly rinsed and drained

1¼ cups water

¼ teaspoon black pepper

¾ teaspoon kosher salt

¼ cup fresh lime juice (from 3 limes)

¼ cup grapeseed oil

3 tablespoons finely chopped fresh cilantro

2 Persian cucumbers, quartered and sliced

6 radishes, halved and sliced

4 cups loosely packed baby arugula

⌣ COOKING TIP ⌣

This is a perfect dish for leftover quinoa as it's served cold.

⌐ VARIATION ⌐

By now you know I love arugula, but feel free to use your favorite leafy green: mâche, spinach, spring mix, etc.

Since I started eating healthier in the past seven to ten years, I've developed a big love for quinoa. It's versatile, so I always try to incorporate it into whatever I'm cooking, from breakfast to desserts. It has a lot of protein and a lot of fiber. I love garnishing it with cilantro, too. Not everyone likes the taste of cilantro, so you can leave it out, but the tangy dressing is a nice balance to this hearty grain. Also, if you don't have grapeseed oil, you can substitute olive oil. This salad can easily be cooked ahead of eating, which also makes it an easy and healthy dish to bring to a potluck.

Quinoa Salad with Cilantro-Lime Dressing

SERVES **4**   HANDS-ON **15 MINUTES**   TOTAL **35 MINUTES**

1 Combine the quinoa, water, pepper, and ¼ teaspoon of the salt in a medium saucepan. Bring to a boil over medium-high; cover and reduce the heat to low. Cook until all the liquid has been absorbed, about 16 minutes. Fluff with a fork, and cool completely. (Spread the quinoa on a large plate or sheet pan to expedite the cooling time.)

2 Whisk together the lime juice, oil, cilantro, and remaining ½ teaspoon salt in a large bowl. Add the cooked quinoa, cucumber slices, radish slices, and arugula; toss to coat. Serve immediately.

Funnily enough, though this salad is one of my favorites, the recipe came about on one of those serendipitous *I'm hungry and going to use up everything left in the fridge* type of days. I always have fennel and arugula around, and I had one green apple left, so I threw it in as a last-minute addition. During apple season I love making this salad as either a starter for dinner, or I'll do it as a full meal when I indulge in the three-cheese crostini. They're basically really amazing croutons.

Arugula, Apple, and Fennel Salad with Citrus Vinaigrette and Three-Cheese Crostini

SERVES **4**   HANDS-ON **15 MINUTES**   TOTAL **20 MINUTES**

1   Preheat the oven to 375°F. Whisk together the shallot, citrus juices, honey, mustard, salt, and white pepper; let stand for 2 minutes. Add the extra-virgin olive oil in a slow, steady stream, whisking until blended. Set aside the dressing.

2   Toss together the arugula, Bibb lettuce, apple, fennel bulb, and walnuts in a large bowl. Set aside the salad.

3   Place the baguette slices in a single layer on a parchment paper-lined baking sheet, and lightly brush the tops with the olive oil. Bake until lightly toasted, about 2 minutes. Remove from the oven.

4   Stir together the cheeses, lemon zest, and black pepper in a small bowl; stir in 1 tablespoon of the reserved chopped fennel fronds. Spoon about 1 tablespoon of the cheese mixture onto each toasted bread slice, and return them to the oven. Bake until the cheese slightly melts and the bread edges are crispy, 2 to 3 minutes.

5   Add the dressing to the salad, and toss. Divide the salad evenly among 4 plates, and serve with 2 crostini.

1 small shallot, finely chopped

1 tablespoon fresh lime juice

1 tablespoon fresh lemon juice

2 teaspoons honey

1 teaspoon Dijon mustard

½ teaspoon kosher salt

¼ teaspoon white pepper

¼ cup extra-virgin olive oil

3 cups baby arugula

1 head Bibb lettuce, torn

1 Granny Smith apple, thinly sliced

1 small fennel bulb, thinly sliced, fronds chopped and reserved

½ cup chopped toasted walnuts

8 (½-inch-thick) baguette bread slices

2 tablespoons olive oil

½ cup ricotta cheese

¼ cup crumbled feta cheese

½ cup shredded mozzarella cheese

½ teaspoon lemon zest

¼ teaspoon black pepper

MAKE AHEAD

The vinaigrette can be made up to a week ahead of time, stored in the fridge in an airtight container. It's a nice dressing to have on hand for any salad.

VARIATION

Feel free to use only arugula or mix up the greens to your liking.

1 medium zucchini, cut into ¾-inch pieces

1 medium yellow squash, cut into ¾-inch pieces

1 Japanese eggplant, cut into ¾-inch pieces

1 (8-ounce) package small button mushrooms, trimmed, sliced

4 medium shallots, halved, plus 1 small shallot, finely chopped

1 tablespoon sherry vinegar

1 tablespoon chopped fresh thyme

½ cup plus 1 tablespoon extra-virgin olive oil

1½ teaspoons kosher salt

¾ teaspoon black pepper

3 tablespoons balsamic vinegar

1 teaspoon honey

1 teaspoon Dijon mustard

1½ cups heirloom cherry tomato halves

1 large head romaine lettuce, torn

1 cup crumbled feta cheese

½ cup loosely packed basil leaves, thinly sliced

I know what you're thinking. Ratatouille and romaine salad don't go together! Okay, I initially thought the same thing because this recipe was actually a mistake. A lovely, delicious mistake, in fact. I used to go to this café in L.A. called the Moustache Café and I always ordered the ratatouille and a romaine salad. When I started working on this book I said, "I want to do a ratatouille and a romaine salad." I guess the fast-talking Italian in me had come out because my team thought I meant to do them together, which wasn't my intention. But then I tried it and thought, *Wow, this is terrific*. I love mixing the heft of the ratatouille with the lightness from the romaine. It's really so good, and you don't need to add protein if you don't want to. Also, I always double the ratatouille recipe and save half to eat with eggs the next morning. Trust me, you'll be happy there's more.

Ratatouille and Romaine Salad with Balsamic Vinaigrette

SERVES **8**   HANDS-ON **20 MINUTES**   TOTAL **1 HOUR, 30 MINUTES**

1 Preheat the oven to 375°F. Line a large rimmed baking sheet with aluminum foil. Place the zucchini, squash, eggplant, mushrooms, shallot halves, sherry vinegar, thyme, ¼ cup of the oil, 1 teaspoon of the salt, and ½ teaspoon of the pepper in a large bowl; toss to combine, coating all the vegetables. Spread the vegetables in a single layer on the prepared baking sheet, and bake until the vegetables are caramelized and softened, 45 to 50 minutes. Remove the vegetables from the pan, and cool to room temperature.

2 Meanwhile, whisk together the balsamic vinegar, chopped shallot, honey, mustard, and remaining ½ teaspoon salt and ¼ teaspoon pepper in a small bowl. Let stand for 2 minutes. Add the remaining 5 tablespoons oil in a slow, steady stream, whisking into the balsamic mixture until blended. Toss together the roasted vegetables and cherry tomatoes with half of the dressing.

3 Place the torn romaine in a large bowl or arrange on a large platter. Spoon the vegetable mixture over the lettuce; sprinkle with the feta and basil. Serve the salad with the remaining dressing.

| MAKE AHEAD |

The vegetables can be roasted a day ahead, and the dressing can be made a day ahead. The variation is perfect for leftover pasta.

⊃ VARIATION ⊂

Prepare 1 cup of uncooked mini penne pasta according to package directions. Cool the pasta completely. Prepare the recipe as directed, adding the cooked and cooled pasta to the vegetable mixture in Step 2.

CHAPTER 3

HAPPY HOUR

Ordinarily, I get home at the end of the day and unwind with a glass of chilled buttery Chardonnay or crisp Sauvignon Blanc. For me, the colder the better. With each sip, I can literally feel my shoulders drop. Pretty soon I'm nestled in a chair, with a cat on my lap, feeling like a wedge of Brie that's been allowed to soften— and that's a good thing.

For parties or a special dinner, though, I like a good cocktail—a sophisticated mixed drink shaken, though sometimes stirred, always chilled, and poured into a lovely glass. Oh, and its effect: refreshing, charming, inspiring, seductive, celebratory, and perfect. I understand why cocktails have enjoyed a resurgence in popularity these past few years. The right spirit casts its own spell on an evening. Before dinner, a good cocktail can stimulate both appetites and conversation. As a digestif, it enables the night to roll to a more gradual conclusion.

Tom and I keep a well-stocked bar in the cozy alcove outside our library for just such occasions. A mint julep on a warm summer afternoon has the effect of a refreshing breeze, and an icy martini sipped ever so slowly can literally stop time. But when it comes to deciding on a drink—not simply a drink but rather the perfect one for the moment—I will often find myself hemming and hawing, trying to remember what I last enjoyed, and what was in it, and wishing I had one of those brilliantly clever cocktail menus I always read at restaurants.

But no longer. With this chapter, I decided to solve that quandary for myself, and hopefully for you, with a small but dependable list of favorites. They range from basic to bubbly, sweet to spicy, and simple to sophisticated. They are perfect for an intimate conversation or elevating the atmosphere when you have a room full of guests and want them to mix and mingle. None is so complicated that you'll pine for a bartender. In fact, the opposite is true.

I have also complemented the spirits menu with a slate of spirited snacks, easy-to-prepare small bites, and peppy dipping sauces. My Happy Hour is even happier when there is a plate of scrumptious edibles.

I carefully chose these recipes for the rave reviews they've received after I served them at my own parties. I mean Goat Cheese and Asparagus Crostini. Bloody Mary Tea Sandwiches. Brown Sugar Sriracha Bacon Bites. I only have to read those recipes and my mouth starts to water. I hope you'll have the same reaction, too.

Bringing the two together is like throwing a party and hiring a live band. The room swings.

Here's the good news: Nothing in this chapter is difficult to make. And here's the even better news: The party is about to start.

Cheers!

Tom and I both feel a kinship with the Southwest, so it's no surprise we both like a fiery burst of flavor in our food. Not the four-alarm blaze that makes your eyes water. I'm talking about a tangy accompaniment that is just enough of a solo performer to make a familiar taste new again, and such is the case here with the dependable margarita. I'm passionate about ginger. My husband can wax poetic about the kick of a ripe jalapeño. Together, these two ingredients pack an invigorating punch. There's just enough tang to energize this potion without having to worry you're going to get burned. The tequila mellows out things, so the heat lies on your tongue but doesn't overpower your taste buds.

Spicy Margarita with Jalapeño and Ginger

SERVES **1**   HANDS-ON **5 MINUTES**   TOTAL **5 MINUTES**

1 Using the back of a wooden spoon, crush together the sea salt and lime zest in a small bowl. Rub the lime wedge around the rim of a margarita glass, and dip the rim in the salt mixture; fill the glass with ice.

2 Muddle the jalapeño and ginger in a cocktail shaker to release the flavors; fill halfway with ice. Add the tequila, lime juice, orange liqueur, and Simple Syrup. Cover with the lid, and shake vigorously until thoroughly chilled, about 30 seconds. Strain into the prepared margarita glass. Garnish with lime wedges and jalapeño slices, if desired.

2 tablespoons sea salt flakes

1 teaspoon lime zest, plus
   1½ tablespoons fresh lime juice

1 lime wedge, plus lime wedges for
   garnish

1 teaspoon minced jalapeño chile, plus
   slices for garnish

3 slices fresh ginger

¼ cup (2 ounces) blanco tequila

1½ tablespoons (¾ ounce) orange
   liqueur (such as Cointreau)

2 tablespoons Simple Syrup (recipe
   follows)

Simple Syrup

MAKES **1 CUP**

Bring the sugar and water to a simmer in a small saucepan over medium; simmer until the sugar has dissolved, about 5 minutes. Cool completely, about 15 minutes. Store in an airtight container in the refrigerator for up to 2 weeks.

1 cup granulated sugar

1 cup water

⌇ COOKING TIP ⌇

When working with jalapeños, it's best to wear gloves. If you don't, wash your hands thoroughly before your hands go anywhere near your eyes. I speak from experience.

INGREDIENT NOTE

The heat of a jalapeño depends on how much of the rib and seeds you keep in. If you want more heat, keep the seeds and ribs. For less heat, chop your jalapeño without seeds or ribs.

Next to lemons, watermelons are my favorite fruit. Their distinctively light, sweet flavor seems to expand in my mouth with a refreshing zeal. They're probably the only thing I love about summer. I make these when Tom has some Southwestern chicken on the grill. The trick is to use seedless watermelons so you can cut them into chunks and toss them directly into the processor. The lime juice enhances the melon; from the moment I add it into the blender, I begin anticipating the combination of tart and sweet. Don't be afraid to improvise. The fruity twist on this standard cocktail opens up a world of possibilities. Think of it as a vacation in a glass.

Watermelon Margaritas

SERVES **4**   HANDS-ON **15 MINUTES**   TOTAL **15 MINUTES**

Process the watermelon, lime juice, and sugar in a blender until very smooth, 3 to 4 minutes. Pour through a fine wire-mesh strainer into a small pitcher. Stir in the tequila and orange liqueur, and pour into 4 ice-filled glasses. Garnish with the watermelon and lime wedges.

⊶ VARIATION ⊷

Make a second pitcher with strawberries instead of the watermelon.

5 cups seedless watermelon chunks plus wedges or balls for garnish

¼ cup fresh lime juice (from about 3 limes) plus lime wedges for garnish

2 tablespoons granulated sugar

¾ cup (6 ounces) blanco tequila

2 tablespoons (1 ounce) orange liqueur (such as Cointreau)

MAKE AHEAD

Planning for a party? Make a pitcher ahead of time—it can keep for up to 2 days in the fridge.

This favorite of mine dates back to when I first came of age to order a cocktail in a restaurant. The sophisticated sound of the name made this drink fun to order ("I'll have a Kir Royale, please"), and made me seem like I knew what I was doing (I didn't). It was served in a tall, elegant flute, which made every occasion feel like a celebration, and still does. And, of course, the light effervescence of this drink—i.e. the bubbles—made me feel grown-up. It's still a favorite before-meal starter, pleasant accompaniment with a weekend brunch, or treat for a late afternoon visit with girlfriends. Though traditionally made with Champagne, I substitute prosecco. This Italian bubbly and the fresh berries dropped in the glasses, along with the cassis, provide a hint of currant flavor that trumpets your taste buds to attention, as is the duty of a first-class aperitif.

1 pint fresh raspberries

1½ to 2 tablespoons (¾ to 1 ounce) crème de cassis

Prosecco, chilled

Berry Kir Royale

SERVES **4**   HANDS-ON **5 MINUTES**   TOTAL **5 MINUTES**

Drop 1 to 3 raspberries in each of 4 Champagne flutes. Add 1 to 1½ teaspoons crème de cassis to each glass. Top each glass with prosecco. Serve immediately.

According to popular lore, this drink dates back to a stormy winter night in the 1940s when a group of air travelers became stranded in a small port town in Ireland. A resourceful bartender provided a double-dose of just what these weary people needed by adding whiskey to coffee, and a classic was born. This drink remains perfect for the nighttime, especially in the winter months when the temperature drops and you want to warm up from the inside out. This particular recipe relies on the tried and true original lineup of coffee, whiskey, and whipped cream, though I've given the latter my own twist with the addition of lemon. Think of this on a cold night by the fire, after a day on the ski slopes, or as a well-deserved reward for shoveling the driveway.

Valerie's Irish Coffee with Lemon-Vanilla Whipped Cream

SERVES **1**   HANDS-ON **10 MINUTES**   TOTAL **10 MINUTES**

1 Make the Irish Coffee: Combine the hot water and brown sugar in a mug; stir until the sugar dissolves. Stir in the whiskey and the desired amount of espresso.

2 Make the Lemon-Vanilla Whipped Cream: Beat the heavy cream, granulated sugar, vanilla, and lemon zest with a heavy-duty electric stand mixer fitted with the whisk attachment on high speed just until soft peaks form.

3 Top the Irish coffee with a generous dollop of the whipped cream, and serve immediately with a spoon.

IRISH COFFEE

2 tablespoons hot water

1 tablespoon brown sugar

3 tablespoons (1½ ounces) Irish whiskey

6 to 7½ tablespoons (3 to 3¾ ounces) hot espresso

LEMON-VANILLA WHIPPED CREAM

1½ cups chilled heavy cream

2 tablespoons granulated sugar

1½ teaspoons vanilla extract

½ teaspoon lemon zest

MAKE AHEAD

The whipped cream can be made a day ahead and kept cold in the fridge. This recipe makes 3 cups, so brew a pot of 6 servings of Irish coffee, or serve the extra cream over your favorite dessert.

2 tablespoons (1 ounce) gin

2 tablespoons (1 ounce) bitter orange liqueur (such as Campari)

2 tablespoons (1 ounce) sweet vermouth

2 tablespoons fresh orange juice

Orange peel strip

This classic cocktail has inspired oodles of print since its inception in a tony Florence bar in the early 1900s when an Italian count with the name Negroni asked the bartender to make his Americano even more potent. Since then, notable admirers include Anthony Bourdain; my dear friend, the gifted chef Ludo Lefebvre; and my husband, Tom. In fact, Ludo and Tom bonded over this special version that includes fresh orange juice in addition to Campari while still relying on the entertaining partnership of gin and vermouth. Ludo makes them in a big pitcher, hence his and Tom's lasting friendship. I prefer a demure pour in a stemmed glass, allowing for an aromatic scent of citrus between sips. I suggest partnering this with inspiring conversation, either before or after dinner, along with the snack mix you'll find on page 101.

Tom and Ludo's Special Negroni

SERVES **1**   HANDS-ON **5 MINUTES**   TOTAL **5 MINUTES**

Fill a cocktail shaker with ice; add the gin, orange liqueur, vermouth, and orange juice. Cover with the lid, and shake vigorously until chilled, about 30 seconds. Strain into an old-fashioned glass with ice, and garnish with the orange peel.

My husband is an aficionado of the Manhattan, a drink that dates back to the late 1800s. He insists on the classic ingredients: bourbon, vermouth, and orange bitters. Stirred at least 30 seconds. And on the rocks (as opposed to the stemmed glass I prefer). His son Tony saw a bartender make a Manhattan with bourbon he'd infused with butter and, knowing his dad's fondness for this tasty refreshment, brought us the idea. We found the butter smoothed out the bourbon in the most delightful manner. It was akin to discovering an enchanting new facet to an old friend. Suddenly we wanted to spend more time together. Though preparation takes a little longer, you keep the butter-infused bourbon in the freezer, and since the alcohol doesn't freeze, you also end up with marvelous bourbon-infused butter that tastes as if it's also been aged in Kentucky barrels. Use it to sauté corn or potatoes or other vegetables. Just don't sauté yourself in the butter-infused bourbon.

Buttery Manhattan

SERVES **1**   HANDS-ON **10 MINUTES**   TOTAL **10 MINUTES**

¼ cup (2 ounces) Butter-Infused Bourbon (recipe follows)

¼ cup (2 ounces) sweet vermouth

Dash of spiced cherry or regular bitters (such as Angostura)

1 orange slice

1 regular or Italian maraschino cherry

Combine the Butter-Infused Bourbon, vermouth, and bitters in a cocktail shaker filled with ice. Cover with the lid, and shake vigorously until chilled, about 30 seconds. Strain into a chilled glass. Serve straight up or on the rocks. Garnish with the orange slice and cherry.

Butter-Infused Bourbon and Bourbon-Infused Butter

MAKES ABOUT **3 CUPS BOURBON** AND **¾ CUP BUTTER**
HANDS-ON **10 MINUTES**   TOTAL **4 HOURS, 10 MINUTES**

1 (750-milliliter) bottle good-quality bourbon (such as Maker's Mark)

1 cup unsalted butter

1   Combine the bourbon and butter in a medium saucepan, and cook, stirring often, over medium just until the butter melts, about 3 minutes. Transfer the mixture to a freezer-safe container, and freeze until the butter has solidified, about 4 hours.

2   Remove the solid bourbon-infused butter, and refrigerate in an airtight container for up to 8 days to use for cooking. Pour the bourbon through a fine wire-mesh strainer lined with a coffee filter into a large pitcher to remove any remaining particles of butter. Return the butter-infused bourbon to its original bottle, and keep frozen for up to 1 month to use in cocktails.

INGREDIENT NOTE
It is important to use unsalted butter here!

MAKE AHEAD

The Butter-Infused Bourbon can be kept in the freezer for up to 1 month; it's great to have on hand whenever you're ready for your Manhattan.

Everyone likes a good party drink, and this twist on the original gin fizz is slightly unconventional without landing anyone in unfamiliar territory. In fact, experience leads me to predict you should prepare for compliments. I like this for the blast of lemon, lime, and rosemary, which refreshes without too much sweetness, and is followed by a revelation of aromatic gin. I make the simple syrup ahead of time and steep the rosemary to ensure a healthy transfer of flavor. The syrup's main purpose is to level the tartness of the lemon-lime juice. I serve this in a rocks glass with ice and add a sprig of freshly cut rosemary from my garden.

Rosemary Gin Fizz

SERVES **1**   HANDS-ON **5 MINUTES**   TOTAL **5 MINUTES**

Combine the gin, simple syrup, lemon juice, and lime juice in a cocktail shaker filled with ice. Cover with the lid, and shake vigorously until thoroughly chilled, about 30 seconds. Strain into a rocks glass filled with ice. Top with the seltzer water, and garnish with the rosemary sprig and lemon slice.

¼ cup (2 ounces) gin

2 tablespoons Rosemary Simple Syrup (recipe follows)

1 tablespoon fresh lemon juice

1 tablespoon fresh lime juice

¼ cup seltzer water

1 small rosemary sprig

Lemon or lime slice

Rosemary Simple Syrup

MAKES **¾ CUP**   HANDS-ON **5 MINUTES**   TOTAL **25 MINUTES**

Stir together the sugar, water, and rosemary sprigs in a small saucepan over medium. Bring to a simmer, and cook, stirring, and gently muddle the rosemary with a wooden spoon, until the sugar has completely dissolved, about 1 minute. Remove from the heat, and cool to room temperature, about 20 minutes. Strain into a small, airtight container, discarding the rosemary, and refrigerate for up to 2 weeks.

¾ cup granulated sugar

¾ cup water

4 rosemary sprigs

My sister-in-law Robin introduced me to this sweet, creamy variation of the classic martini (a grown-up and delicious reworking of that treat). It tastes like a slice of Key lime pie, only the vanilla liqueur makes it the most unforgettable Key lime pie you'll have ever tasted. It's usually made with cream or half-and-half, but the coconut milk perfectly balances the tartness of lime. Rimming the glass with graham cracker crumbs is an inspired little touch that finishes this whimsical presentation and makes for an unforgettable splurge. Get ready to pucker up and enjoy!

Key Lime Martini

SERVES **1** HANDS-ON **10 MINUTES** TOTAL **10 MINUTES**

1 lime wedge, plus more for garnish

1 graham cracker sheet, finely crushed

¼ cup (2 ounces) vodka

2 tablespoons (1 ounce) Licor 43 liqueur

2 tablespoons (1 ounce) fresh lime juice

2 tablespoons (1 ounce) coconut milk

2 tablespoons (1 ounce) orange juice

SERVING TIP

This beautiful cocktail should be consumed immediately after the freshly strained liquor filters into the glass. If left to sit, the creamer separates from the lime juice, and curdles lightly, losing both its essence and its visual appeal.

1 Rub the lime wedge around the rim of a martini glass.

2 Place the graham cracker crumbs in a small saucer, and dip the rim of the prepared glass in the crumbs to coat the rim; freeze the prepared glass 5 to 10 minutes while preparing the drink.

3 Combine the vodka, Licor 43, lime juice, coconut milk, and orange juice in a cocktail shaker filled with ice. Cover with the lid, and shake vigorously until thoroughly chilled, about 30 seconds. Strain the mixture into the prepared martini glass, and garnish with a lime wedge. Serve immediately.

BLUE CHEESE-STUFFED
OLIVE MARTINI
PG 96

KEY LIME MARTINI
PG 92

SPRITZ MARTINI
PG 97

1 teaspoon good-quality blue cheese or
Roquefort cheese, softened

2 large green olives, pitted

½ teaspoon dry vermouth

6 tablespoons (3 ounces) vodka

| MAKE AHEAD |

The olives can be stuffed and kept in the fridge for up to 4 days.

There's little to say about the martini that hasn't already been said in books, songs, and dimly lit corners of sophisticated bars, other than to restate the consensus opinion: This marvel of simplicity is perfection in a glass. "Cool and clean," as Hemingway wrote. Indeed, I love an icy-cold martini, and prefer mine dry, though not as dry as playwright Noel Coward, who said the perfect martini was entirely gin and merely pointed in the direction of Italy. If blue cheese olives are involved, I'm all in. Though available in stores, I have never liked the quality of the blue cheese. I like a really good blue cheese, so I stuff my own olives. I highly recommend this. It's easy and adds a personal touch that makes the moment I plop the olive in my mouth a tasty exclamation point to this exquisite treat.

Blue Cheese-Stuffed Olive Martini

SERVES **1**   HANDS-ON **5 MINUTES**   TOTAL **15 MINUTES**

1 Using a small spoon, pastry bag, or plastic bag with a corner cut off, insert ½ teaspoon of the blue cheese into each olive.

2 Pour the vermouth into a martini glass, and swirl to coat. Freeze the glass until chilled, about 10 minutes.

3 When ready to serve, add the vodka to a cocktail shaker filled with ice. Cover with the lid, and shake vigorously until thoroughly chilled, about 30 seconds. Strain into the prepared martini glass, and garnish with the stuffed olives.

Tom and I were vacationing in Italy the first time I tried an Aperol Spritz. Whether we were in Rome, Venice, or my favorite city, San Gimignano, I saw people in restaurants and cafes sipping this vibrantly colored refreshment. One afternoon we came back from sightseeing and I finally ordered a spritz. It was served in a goblet with lots of ice and fruit, and with my first sip our vacation soared to a new level of *meraviglioso.* Tom thought it would be better to punch it up a bit with a shot of vodka. The bartender reluctantly obliged. Since then, I rejiggered the traditional recipe so it can be prepared straight up, as a martini. You spike with vodka, shake, and top with a spritz of prosecco. Trust me, this icy-cold favorite of mine will turn a warm afternoon or evening into a special Italian sojourn.

Spritz Martini

SERVES **1**   HANDS-ON **5 MINUTES**   TOTAL **35 MINUTES**

1 small orange wedge

¼ cup (2 ounces) vodka

2 tablespoons (1 ounce) Aperol

4 to 6 tablespoons (2 to 3 ounces) chilled prosecco

Orange peel twist

1 Freeze a martini glass for 30 minutes. Remove the glass from the freezer, and immediately rub the orange wedge around the rim of the glass.

2 Combine the vodka and Aperol in a cocktail shaker filled with ice. Cover with the lid, and shake vigorously until thoroughly chilled, about 30 seconds. Strain into the prepared glass. Top with chilled prosecco to taste. Garnish with the orange peel twist, and serve immediately.

↑ **VALERIE'S FAMILY CREST**

For years, my son wanted to know if we had a family crest. To me, the names Bertinelli and Van Halen didn't sound like people who would have a family crest. But I went on the show *Who Do You Think You Are*, found a tie on my mother's side to the Claypools, a family dating to William the Conqueror, and lo and behold, I brought back a family crest. My mom, a lifelong painter, put it into a watercolor, which is my favorite medium, and gave it to all of her children. It hangs in my home—and now Wolfie has it, too.

2 tablespoons unsalted butter

2½ cups raw shelled pepitas (pumpkin seeds)

2 tablespoons granulated sugar

½ teaspoon ground cinnamon

½ teaspoon ground ginger

¼ teaspoon ground allspice

¼ teaspoon ground cloves

¼ teaspoon kosher salt

I roast nuts all the time, either on the stove or in the oven. They're a healthy snack and I think they have a cool, decorative look when kept in a beautiful bowl on the kitchen counter or in a clear, classic canning jar. I'm all about simplicity and ease, and that's the case here. Pepitas are pumpkin seeds—the edible part. I harvest them directly from pumpkins during carving season, but more often than not, I buy them raw in the market and then spice them up with a mixture of sugar and salt (feel free to experiment with different spices—for instance, I alternate between cardamom, which I love, and nutmeg, another favorite). As they roast, you can hear them pop. It's like they're singing, "Ready!" Set these pepitas out during cocktail hour and watch them disappear by the handful. I also add them to creamy pumpkin or squash soups and toss them into salads. I never run out of ideas for these guys.

Spiced Pepitas

SERVES **10**   HANDS-ON **5 MINUTES**   TOTAL **30 MINUTES**

1 Preheat the oven to 400°F. Line a rimmed baking sheet with aluminum foil, and lightly grease the foil with cooking spray.

2 Melt the butter in a small skillet or sauté pan over medium. Remove from the heat, and add the pepitas; toss to coat. Stir in the sugar, cinnamon, ginger, allspice, cloves, and salt. Spread the pepitas in an even layer on the prepared baking sheet.

3 Bake until golden brown, 8 to 10 minutes, stirring once or twice during baking. Cool completely, about 15 minutes.

Nothing fancy but impossibly addictive, this old-fashioned snack is included here for sentimental reasons. My mom made this for my dad's weekly poker games. She used Corn, Wheat, and Rice Chex, peanuts, and pretzels. My job was to carry the bowls into the game. I now make my own variation with wasabi peas, mixed nuts, ramen mix, melted butter, and other goodies (though you can substitute fun ingredients until you find your own magic mix). When I bring it out during a football game, or a family gathering, or before a party, my husband literally whimpers, "Please, please, don't do this to me." It's the happiest protest you've ever heard. One secret I insist on: Always use the honey-sweetened corn cereal for that little extra sweet 'n' salty combination. And one other secret: Double the recipe and watch the smiles when they ask for more.

Mom's Amped-Up Snack Mix

SERVES **12 TO 15**   HANDS-ON **10 MINUTES**   TOTAL **35 MINUTES**

1 Preheat the oven to 300°F. Line 2 large rimmed baking sheets with parchment paper. Break the noodles from the ramen noodle soup mix into small pieces, and reserve the seasoning packet for use in Step 3.

2 Stir together the cereal, cheese cracker chips, pretzels, peas, nuts, and ramen noodle pieces in a large bowl.

3 Stir the reserved seasoning packet from the ramen noodle soup mix into the melted butter. Pour over the cereal mixture, and toss to coat. Spread the mixture evenly between the prepared baking sheets.

4 Bake until golden brown, about 12 minutes. Cool completely, about 10 minutes, before serving.

1 package oriental-flavor ramen noodle soup mix

3 cups honey-sweetened corn cereal squares

3 cups Cheddar cheese crispy cracker chips

2 cups mini pretzel twists

1 cup wasabi peas

1 cup mixed nuts

½ cup unsalted butter, melted

MAKE AHEAD

This is another great party dish that can be prepped and kept for up to 5 days in an airtight container.

VARIATION

If this is for a kids' party and the wasabi peas are too strong, leave them out and add another cup of the mixed nuts or goldfish grahams.

BAKED BRIE WITH
ALMONDS AND MANGO
PG 104

SPICED PEPITAS
PG 100

MOM'S AMPED-UP
SNACK MIX
PG 101

½ (17.5-ounce) package frozen puff pastry, thawed

¼ cup mango chutney

¼ cup golden raisins

5 tablespoons toasted slivered almonds

1 (8-ounce) Brie round

1 large egg

1 teaspoon water

Fresh thyme sprigs

2 large apples, sliced

1 French baguette, sliced (optional)

INGREDIENT NOTE
Mango chutney is usually in the international food aisle of your local grocer—if you can't find it, any chutney will do.

I discovered the indulgent buttery goodness of baked Brie sometime in the late 1970s or early 1980s. I had a passion for cooking but little technique and less experience, and I made a version of this dish for the first time in my toaster oven, without the bread. I sautéed almonds and served with sliced apples on the side. Later, the first time I made it with bread, I didn't close the dough tight enough and the cheese oozed out while the dough crisped up, like toast. It didn't look pretty, but it was amazingly good. And this recipe is even better. You can serve this with apple slices, pear slices, or celery sticks. Buttery crackers will do the trick, too. I suggest using the puff pastry to bring this sweet, crunchy treat to your mouth one bite at a time. Simply decadent, this dish is perfect either before a special meal or for dessert. There's one last step: Prepare for compliments.

Baked Brie with Almonds and Mango

SERVES **8**   HANDS-ON **10 MINUTES**   TOTAL **35 MINUTES**

1 Preheat the oven to 425°F. Line a rimmed baking sheet with parchment paper.

2 Place the pastry sheet on a lightly floured work surface, and roll into a 10-inch square. Spread the chutney over the pastry; sprinkle with the raisins and almonds. Place the Brie round in the center of the dough. Fold the dough up and over the cheese and fillings, pleating the dough to enclose like a packet or purse. Trim the dough, if needed. Flip the packet over, and place on the prepared baking sheet.

3 Whisk together the egg and water; brush the Brie packet with the egg mixture.

4 Bake until golden, about 20 minutes. Remove from the oven, and sprinkle with the thyme. Cool about 3 minutes, and serve with the fresh apple slices and/or sliced baguette.

I enjoy a good, crisp, flavorful cracker: newfangled flatbreads, rice cakes, popadums, as well as my childhood favorites Triscuits, Wheat Thins, and Cheez-Its. One day I decided to make my own and they were quick and easy. I threw all the ingredients in the food processor, rolled out the dough while it was still moist, and cut it into imprecise rectangles. The best part was seasoning them exactly as I wanted—and I experimented. Some got a heavy dose of freshly ground black pepper, others were laden with Parmesan, others got a dash of rosemary, and the rest got the whole shebang. You can make these to taste. I served them to a girlfriend one afternoon with a plate of cheese, and soon she dispensed with the cheese and just nibbled the crackers, explaining, "These are addictive little buggers."

Rosemary and Pepper Crackers

SERVES **6**   HANDS-ON **15 MINUTES**   TOTAL **30 MINUTES**

1 Preheat the oven to 400°F. Line a baking sheet with parchment paper.

2 Process the flour, Parmesan, rosemary, black pepper, cayenne pepper, and ½ teaspoon of the salt in a food processor until combined, 5 or 6 times. Add the butter, and pulse until incorporated. Add ¼ cup of the cream, and process until the dough pulls away from the sides and forms a ball. (If a ball does not form, add up to 2 tablespoons cream, 1 teaspoon at a time, and process until the dough comes together.)

3 Pat the dough into a flat rectangle on a lightly floured surface; sprinkle the dough with flour, and roll into a 12- x 8-inch rectangle (about ¼ inch thick). Sprinkle with the remaining ½ teaspoon salt, gently pressing to adhere. Cut the dough into ½-inch squares, and carefully transfer to the prepared baking sheet.

4 Bake until light golden brown, 8 to 10 minutes. Cool completely on the baking sheet on a wire rack, 10 to 12 minutes.

1¼ cups all-purpose flour, plus more for dusting

½ cup grated Parmesan cheese

1 teaspoon minced fresh rosemary

½ teaspoon coarsely ground black pepper

¼ teaspoon cayenne pepper

1 teaspoon kosher salt

¼ cup cold unsalted butter, cut into ½-inch pieces

4 to 6 tablespoons heavy cream

ROSEMARY AND
PEPPER CRACKERS
PG 105

Asparagus is loaded with fiber; vitamins A, C, E, and K; and a handful of minerals, making it one of the healthiest vegetables. It's also touted for its antioxidants and potential to boost memory and slow the aging process. In other words, these slender stalks offer much more than the versatility I love. I start roasting asparagus as soon as it begins appearing in my farmers' market in the early spring; it heralds a favorite time of year. Inevitably, I have leftovers, and if I don't want them in my eggs the next morning, I make this wonderful pesto dip with feta and Cheddar cheeses. An abundance of herbs keeps it fresh and light tasting. The lemon-pepper panko adds a textural element and lemony verve for a fresh-tasting crowd-pleaser.

Roasted Asparagus Pesto Dip

SERVES **8**   HANDS-ON **15 MINUTES**   TOTAL **30 MINUTES**

1 Preheat the oven to 400°F. Place the asparagus on a rimmed baking sheet. Drizzle with the olive oil; sprinkle with the salt and pepper. Bake until slightly softened and lightly charred, about 10 minutes. Cool 10 minutes. Keep the oven on at 400°F.

2 Meanwhile, process the feta, Cheddar, mayonnaise, basil, parsley, mint, lemon zest, lemon juice, and garlic in a food processor until the herbs are uniformly chopped and the ingredients are well combined. Add the asparagus, and process until roughly chopped.

3 Spoon the mixture into a lightly greased 1-quart baking dish. Stir together the panko and melted butter; sprinkle over the asparagus mixture. Bake until the mixture is warmed through and slightly bubbly and the panko is light golden brown, about 15 minutes. Serve with the crackers or crudités.

1 pound fresh asparagus, trimmed

1 tablespoon olive oil

¼ teaspoon kosher salt

¼ teaspoon black pepper

1 cup crumbled feta cheese

1 cup shredded white Cheddar cheese

½ cup mayonnaise

½ cup firmly packed fresh basil leaves

¼ cup firmly packed fresh flat-leaf parsley leaves

¼ cup firmly packed fresh mint leaves

½ teaspoon lemon zest, plus 1 tablespoon fresh lemon juice (from 1 lemon)

2 garlic cloves, chopped

½ cup lemon-pepper panko (Japanese-style breadcrumbs)

1 tablespoon unsalted butter, melted

Crackers or crudités

2 (15-ounce) cans chickpeas, drained and rinsed

½ cup jarred roasted red bell peppers, drained

3 tablespoons tahini

1 garlic clove, chopped

3 to 4 tablespoons fresh lemon juice (from about 2 lemons)

½ teaspoon kosher salt

5 tablespoons olive oil

Freshly ground black pepper

Pita chips, celery sticks, carrot sticks, halved radishes, green beans, snow peas

I began making my own hummus about 20 years ago and have not stopped. Why? It's a consistent winner. Whenever I have my book group over, for instance, I make hummus and serve it with crudités. The big question among my friends is what flavor I'll make. Over the years I have used roasted carrots, garlic, artichoke, and avocado, but here I have chosen my favorite, roasted red pepper. It's easy to make as I always have tahini in the fridge and chickpeas in the pantry, the main ingredients. Add olive oil and red peppers, and then let the food processor do all the work. It's creamy, with a mild red pepper flavor and a hint of garlic that you can adjust by seasoning to taste. I serve with carrots, celery, radishes, and pita chips; because I'm a nut about utilizing leftovers, any extra hummus can be spread on a turkey sandwich in place of mayonnaise or mustard.

Roasted Red Pepper Hummus

SERVES **6**   HANDS-ON **15 MINUTES**   TOTAL **15 MINUTES**

Process the chickpeas, roasted red peppers, tahini, garlic, lemon juice, and salt in a food processor until the chickpeas are chopped, about 6 times. With the processor running, pour the olive oil through the food chute, and process until a smooth paste forms. Transfer to a bowl, sprinkle with pepper, and serve with the pita chips, celery sticks, carrots sticks, radishes, green beans, and snow peas.

MAKE AHEAD

This can be made up to a day ahead and kept in the fridge if you're in party prep mode.

As far as I'm concerned, I can put anything on top of a piece of toasted bread, place it under the broiler, and it's going to taste good. But when I spread this combination—goat cheese and asparagus—the level of deliciousness ratchets up to an eleven or twelve. Grilling the asparagus takes time, and you can enhance the goat cheese with chives or other herbs. Otherwise, the biggest task with this dish is paying careful attention while it's under the broiler. The fresh tomato adds a final touch that makes this crusty, creamy appetizer full of spring-like flavor. It's very simple to prepare and a crowd-pleaser when served by itself or with other hors d'oeuvres.

Goat Cheese and Asparagus Crostini

SERVES **4**   HANDS-ON **20 MINUTES**   TOTAL **40 MINUTES**

1 Preheat a grill pan over medium-high; preheat the broiler with the oven rack 6 to 8 inches from the heat.

2 Drizzle the asparagus with ½ tablespoon of the olive oil. Toss to coat, and sprinkle with the salt and pepper. Place in the grill pan, and cook until tender and grill marks appear, 3 to 5 minutes per side, depending on the thickness of the asparagus. Remove from the grill pan, and cool 10 minutes. Cut into 2- to 3-inch pieces (about the size of the bread slices).

3 Brush the bread on both sides with the remaining 2 tablespoons oil, and place in a single layer on a baking sheet. Rub the garlic clove all over 1 side of each slice. Broil until golden and crispy, about 2 minutes per side. Remove from the oven, and cool 15 minutes.

4 Divide the goat cheese evenly among the bread slices; top each with 2 to 3 pieces of the grilled asparagus and a few of the cherry tomatoes. Return the bread slices to the oven, and broil just until the cheese is melted, about 2 minutes.

12 fresh asparagus spears, trimmed

2½ tablespoons extra-virgin olive oil

½ teaspoon kosher salt

¼ teaspoon black pepper

12 diagonally cut baguette slices

1 garlic clove

¾ cup goat cheese, softened (about 6 ounces)

1 cup cherry tomatoes, halved

1 (8-ounce) package cream cheese, softened

¼ cup pimiento-stuffed green olives, drained and finely chopped

¼ cup finely chopped celery (about 1 stalk)

½ tablespoon Cajun seasoning

½ teaspoon anchovy paste

½ teaspoon lemon zest

10 white sandwich bread slices

10 whole-wheat sandwich bread slices

40 (⅛-inch-thick) plum tomato slices (4 to 5 medium plum tomatoes)

2 cups loosely packed baby arugula

Pickled okra or pickled jalapeños (optional)

◇ VARIATION ◇

Make it a bloody bull tea sammie by adding a thin slice of roast beef.

When it's tea time, don't offer me tea. But I will spark to a plate of cute tea sandwiches. Who doesn't love a good tea sandwich? I was in London the first time I encountered formal tea sandwiches. They were presented on a multitiered tower with small china plates. The serving was exquisite, and the sandwiches were beyond: smoked salmon, herbed butter and cucumber, egg salad and watercress. It's more than 30 years later and not only do I remember marveling over the cute, bite-size delicacies, I can still taste them. Soft. Fresh. Mmm. With Cajun-flavored cream cheese, fresh tomatoes, and arugula in tender white bread, this recipe is a fun twist on the tomato and cheese sandwich—and the pickled okra is a secret favorite of mine that provides a smile-inducing zest. Super easy, this is a nice surprise with a cocktail.

Bloody Mary Tea Sandwiches
SERVES **10**   HANDS-ON **20 MINUTES**   TOTAL **20 MINUTES**

1 Stir together the cream cheese, olives, celery, Cajun seasoning, anchovy paste, and lemon zest in a medium bowl until well blended.

2 Place the white bread slices on a work surface, and spread about 2 tablespoons of the cream cheese mixture on each slice. Place the wheat bread slices on the work surface; top each with 4 of the tomato slices in a single layer, and add a few arugula leaves. Place 1 white bread slice, cream cheese-side down, on each prepared wheat bread slice.

3 Using a serrated knife, remove the crusts from the sandwiches with a gentle sawing motion, and cut into 40 triangular tea sandwiches.

4 Cover with plastic wrap, and chill until ready to serve. Garnish each tea sandwich with a piece of pickled okra or a pickled jalapeño, if desired.

The secret to making your own pretzels is having the patience to make your own pretzels. I promise you, though, the investment is worth it. The first time I made these was with Duff Goldman, the well-deserved Ace of Cakes, and he made it seem so easy. His encouragement inspired me to give it a try on my own. They are fun to make, and even better with your kids. The only thing to think about ahead of time is whether you want them as an appetizer, snack, or dessert. The Nutella is wonderful when these are soft and warm, but you can substitute a mustard sauce and add sea salt after brushing on the butter before baking. Either way, these are a treat.

Soft Pretzels with Chocolate-Hazelnut Dip

SERVES **8**   HANDS-ON **45 MINUTES**   TOTAL **2 HOURS**

1 cup warm water (about 110°F)

1 tablespoon granulated sugar

1 teaspoon kosher salt

1 (¼-ounce) envelope active dry yeast

5 tablespoons unsalted butter, melted

2¾ cups all-purpose flour, plus more for dusting

¼ cup baking soda

½ cup whole milk

1 cup chocolate-hazelnut spread (such as Nutella)

1   Combine the warm water, sugar, and salt in a large bowl. Stir in the yeast, and let stand until foamy, about 5 minutes. Stir in 3 tablespoons of the melted butter. Add the flour, and stir with a wooden spoon until the dough starts to come together.

2   Turn the dough out onto a lightly floured surface. Knead until the dough is smooth and elastic, about 5 minutes. Place in a lightly greased bowl, turning to grease the top. Cover the dough with plastic wrap, and let rise in a warm place (80°F to 85°F), free from drafts, until almost doubled in bulk, about 1 hour.

3   Preheat the oven to 475°F with the racks in the upper third and lower third of the oven. Lightly grease 2 baking sheets.

4   Cut the dough into 8 pieces. Roll each piece into a 20-inch-long rope. Holding 1 end of the dough rope in each hand, make a U-shape on the floured surface. Leaving about a 3-inch tail on each end, cross the dough ends. Cross the ends again, twisting them together much like a twist tie. Bring the 3-inch tails down, and attach to the dough under the bottom of the U-shape (1 end at about 5 o'clock and the other at about 7 o'clock), forming the shape of a pretzel. Repeat with the remaining dough ropes.

5   Fill a large, wide pot with about 3 inches of water, and add the baking soda. Bring to a brisk simmer over medium-high. Boil the pretzels, 2 at a time, until puffed and shiny, about 2 minutes, transferring to the prepared baking sheets as they are ready. Brush the pretzels with the remaining 2 tablespoons melted butter.

6   Bake the pretzels, switching the baking sheets top rack to bottom rack halfway through, until deeply browned, about 12 minutes.

7   While the pretzels are baking, heat the milk in a small saucepan over medium until the milk just begins to bubble, about 4 minutes. Whisk in the chocolate-hazelnut spread.

8   Serve the warm pretzels with the chocolate-hazelnut dipping sauce.

During my first marriage, my husband's mother, Mrs. Van Halen, made amazing Indonesian meals. The one that stands out most—or rather, the one that's lingered on my taste buds for more than three decades—is her Gado-Gado, a vegetable dish she served with a peanut sauce that literally stopped time. I savored every molecule of its peanuty goodness. Years later, I served her peanut sauce with chicken satay, making for an easy appetizer with bold flavor. She never shared her exact recipe, but I've re-created it as best I can—and I think I got very close. It's exotic but still approachable—and just might cause you to dance the night away. Haha, see what I did there?

Chicken Satay with Peanut Sauce
SERVES **4**   HANDS-ON **25 MINUTES**   TOTAL **2 HOURS, 25 MINUTES**

MRS. VH'S PEANUT SAUCE

1½ tablespoons peanut oil

¼ cup finely chopped yellow onion

1 jalapeño chile (or more), ribs and seeds removed, finely chopped

4 garlic cloves, grated or mashed to a paste with the side of a knife

1½ tablespoons grated fresh ginger

1 cup coconut milk

½ cup creamy natural peanut butter

6 tablespoons fresh lime juice (from about 3 limes)

2 tablespoons sambal oelek (ground fresh chile paste)

2 tablespoons reduced-sodium soy sauce

1 teaspoon fish sauce

SATAY

⅓ cup coconut milk

3 tablespoons vegetable oil

2 tablespoons fresh lime juice

2 tablespoons light brown sugar

1 tablespoon reduced-sodium soy sauce

1 tablespoon fish sauce

1 tablespoon grated fresh ginger

1 teaspoon curry powder

2 garlic cloves, roughly chopped

2 boneless, skinless chicken breasts (about 1 pound)

12 wooden skewers, soaked in water 20 minutes and drained

1 Make the Peanut Sauce: Heat the peanut oil in a small skillet or sauté pan over medium-low. Add the onion and jalapeño, and cook, stirring occasionally, until softened and fragrant, about 5 minutes. Add the garlic and ginger, and cook, stirring constantly, 30 seconds. Remove from the heat, and cool 3 minutes; transfer to a large bowl. Add the coconut milk, peanut butter, lime juice, chile paste, soy sauce, and fish sauce; whisk until smooth. Set aside.

2 Make the Satay: Whisk together the coconut milk, vegetable oil, lime juice, brown sugar, soy sauce, fish sauce, ginger, curry powder, and garlic in a medium bowl. Cut each chicken breast on the diagonal into 6 strips. Place the chicken between 2 sheets of plastic wrap, and flatten to ¼-inch thickness, using a rolling pin or flat side of a meat mallet.

3 Place the chicken strips in a large ziplock freezer bag, and add the coconut milk mixture. Seal the bag, and turn to coat. Chill for 2 to 6 hours.

4 Preheat a grill to medium-high (about 450°F). Remove the chicken from the marinade; discard the marinade. Thread 1 chicken strip onto each skewer. Grill, uncovered, until the chicken is cooked through and lightly charred in places, 2 to 3 minutes per side. Serve with the peanut sauce.

INGREDIENT NOTE
Don't be afraid of fish sacue, as I once was. It adds a depth of flavor that salt just can't give.

⚬ VARIATION ⚬

Want it spicy? Leave in the ribs and seeds of the jalapeño.

Whenever my sister-in-law Robin visits, she brings a few new recipes she thinks I'll like and we end up in the kitchen cooking the whole time. This recipe for Southwestern egg rolls with salsa dipping sauce was an instant hit! It's basically a Tex-Mex mini-burrito—black beans with cheese, corn, scallions, and a yummy gust of spiciness—masquerading in egg roll wrappers as a Chinese appetizer. My stepson Dominic loves the salsa. Leftovers get scooped up with tortilla chips. A tiny tip: As you pulse the tomatoes, garlic, and jalapeños, add the scallions and cilantro to the mixture towards the end, and then dip away! I like that these are baked, not fried; they come out of the oven light and healthy. This is always a hit at parties or as a festive little dinner starter.

Southwestern Egg Rolls with Salsa Dipping Sauce

SERVES **10**   HANDS-ON **20 MINUTES**   TOTAL **45 MINUTES**

1 Make the Egg Rolls: Preheat the oven to 425°F. Spray a rimmed baking sheet generously with cooking spray.

2 Stir together the cheese, corn, beans, spinach, chiles, scallions, cumin, chili powder, cayenne pepper, and salt in a large bowl, making sure to break up any clumps of spinach.

3 Have a small bowl of water ready for moistening your fingers.

4 Place 1 egg roll wrapper on the work surface with 1 corner pointing up and the opposite corner pointing down. Brush the water around the outer edge of the wrapper. Spoon ¼ cup of the filling mixture in the center of the wrapper. Fold the left and right corners over the filling; fold the bottom corner over the filling. Tightly roll the filled end toward the top corner; gently press to seal. Place on the prepared baking sheet. Repeat with the remaining egg roll wrappers and filling.

5 Brush the tops and sides of the egg rolls generously with the beaten egg.

6 Bake until golden brown, 25 to 30 minutes.

7 Meanwhile, make the Salsa: Process the tomatoes, garlic, and jalapeño in a food processor until the tomatoes are almost smooth, about 3 times. Add the scallions, cilantro, lime juice, and salt; pulse just until combined, about 3 times. Serve with the egg rolls.

EGG ROLLS

2½ cups shredded Mexican 4-cheese blend

2 cups frozen corn, thawed

1 (15-ounce) can black beans, drained and rinsed

1 (10-ounce) package frozen chopped spinach, thawed and squeezed dry

1 (4-ounce) can diced green chiles, drained

4 scallions, chopped

1 teaspoon ground cumin

½ teaspoon chili powder

¼ teaspoon cayenne pepper

1½ teaspoons kosher salt

1 (16-ounce) package egg roll wrappers

1 large egg, lightly beaten

SALSA

5 plum tomatoes, quartered

1 small garlic clove, minced

½ jalapeño chile, seeded and finely chopped

3 scallions, white and light green parts only, finely chopped

1 cup loosely packed cilantro leaves and stems, finely chopped

2 teaspoons fresh lime juice

2 teaspoons kosher salt

MAKE AHEAD

Both the filling and salsa can be made ahead of time and kept in the fridge.

Back when we had a house in Park City, Utah, we frequented an Italian restaurant so often they put a sign above our regular table that said, "Wolfie's Booth." The reason we were at the restaurant so often? Their bacon-wrapped jalapeño shrimp. (Hold on a moment while I savor the memory of them. Seriously, my mouth is watering.) Sadly, the restaurant closed before I was able to get their recipe, so I developed this particular one on my own and have tinkered with it over the years to the point where I look for excuses to make it. A party, Sunday night football, a birthday, Tuesday night . . . I'm in, and so is my entire family, along with a few of my neighbors. The sauce is sweet with a hint of Cherry Coke, and once it connects with the jalapeño, it sits on the tongue with an exciting contrast of hot and sweet and savory. It goes well with a cold cocktail or even a light beer. These will disappear quickly.

Bacon-Wrapped Jalapeño Shrimp with Cherry Cola BBQ Sauce

SERVES **16**   HANDS-ON **35 MINUTES**   TOTAL **45 MINUTES**

CHERRY COLA BBQ SAUCE

1½ tablespoons bacon drippings

½ large red onion, chopped (about 1 cup)

2 garlic cloves, chopped

½ teaspoon kosher salt

½ teaspoon garlic powder

¼ teaspoon dry mustard

2 cups cherry cola soft drink

½ cup red wine vinegar

1 cup ketchup

SHRIMP

16 extra-large shrimp, peeled, deveined, and tails removed (about 12 ounces)

1 jalapeño chile, stem removed, seeded, and cut lengthwise into 16 thin strips

1 teaspoon kosher salt

1 teaspoon black pepper

8 bacon slices, halved crosswise

> ### MAKE AHEAD
>
> The BBQ sauce will hold up to 2 weeks in the fridge. If you're prepping for a party, the shrimp can be wrapped ahead of time and cooked later.

◆ TRICK TECHNIQUE ◆

If you're someone who loves their bacon in the morning, start saving the drippings in a jar for uses like this one!

1 Make the BBQ Sauce: Heat the bacon drippings in a small saucepan over medium-high. Add the onion, and cook, stirring occasionally, until softened, about 5 minutes. Add the chopped garlic, and cook, stirring often, for 1 minute. Stir in the salt, garlic powder, and dry mustard, and cook, stirring often, until the spices are toasted and fragrant and the onions are a deep maroon color, about 2 minutes. Whisk in the cherry cola and vinegar, and cook, stirring often, about 2 minutes. Stir in the ketchup. Bring the sauce to a boil, and cook until reduced to about 2 cups and the mixture coats the back of a spoon, 12 to 15 minutes.

2 Meanwhile, make the Shrimp: Heat a cast-iron skillet or grill pan over medium. Cut a long ¼-inch-deep slit in the inner curve of each shrimp; insert 1 jalapeño strip. Sprinkle with the salt and pepper. Wrap each shrimp tightly with 1 bacon piece. Set on a plate, seam sides down.

3 Place the bacon-wrapped shrimp, seam sides down, in the hot skillet, and cook, turning occasionally, until the bacon is crisp and the shrimp are just cooked through, 5 to 6 minutes. Serve the shrimp with the BBQ sauce.

When I begin to think about the many reasons I treasure my friendship with the incomparable, irrepressible Betty White, one of them is the way her face lights up when we're at a restaurant and she looks down the menu and sees short ribs. Betty is a woman of many passions and loves, and one of them is short ribs. When I invited her on my cooking show, I had to make this favorite of hers. You can't disappoint Betty, and this recipe won't disappoint you. These short ribs are ridiculously tender, flavorful, and delicious—two bites of heaven. The crunchy, creamy cheese toast is a perfect contrast to the short rib and an inspired way to get the meaty morsel to your mouth, where, I guarantee, it will melt—the same effect spending time with Betty has on my heart.

Glazed Short Rib Stacks

SERVES **4** HANDS-ON **40 MINUTES** TOTAL **1 HOUR, 55 MINUTES**

1 Cut the short ribs into 12 bite-size pieces. Sprinkle with the salt, paprika, and ¼ teaspoon of the pepper. Heat the olive oil in a small Dutch oven over medium. Add the short rib pieces, and cook, turning to brown all over, about 4 to 5 minutes. Remove from the Dutch oven.

2 Add the onion, carrot, garlic, and thyme to the Dutch oven, and cook until the vegetables just begin to brown, about 2 minutes. Add the wine, and increase the heat to medium-high. Bring to a boil, and cook until the liquid is reduced to about ⅓ cup, 1 to 2 minutes. Add the short rib pieces, broth, honey, and vinegar, and reduce the heat to a low simmer. Cover and cook until the beef is tender but not falling apart, about 1 hour and 15 minutes. Using a slotted spoon, transfer the beef and vegetables to a large platter.

3 Preheat the oven to 400°F. Remove and discard the vegetables and thyme sprig from the beef mixture.

4 Increase the heat to high, and bring the liquid in the Dutch oven to a boil. Boil until the liquid is reduced to about 1 cup, about 2 minutes. Return the beef to the Dutch oven, and toss to coat. Remove from the heat, and cover to keep warm.

5 Place the baguette slices in a single layer on a baking sheet, and bake until just crisp but not browned, 4 to 5 minutes. Increase the oven temperature to broil.

6 Place the cream cheese, blue cheese, 1 tablespoon chopped chives, and remaining ¼ teaspoon pepper in a small bowl, and mash until combined. Spread about 1 tablespoon of the mixture on each toast, and broil until the cheese mixture just begins to brown, 1 to 2 minutes.

7 Top each cheese toast with 1 tomato slice and 1 piece of the glazed short rib. Garnish with the chopped chives and thyme.

SHORT RIBS

1 pound boneless beef short ribs, trimmed

1 teaspoon kosher salt

½ teaspoon sweet paprika

½ teaspoon black pepper

1 tablespoon extra-virgin olive oil

1 small yellow onion, quartered

1 medium carrot, cut into large chunks

6 garlic cloves, crushed

1 thyme sprig, plus more for garnish

½ cup dry red wine

1½ cups reduced-sodium beef broth

2 tablespoons honey

1 tablespoon balsamic vinegar

ADDITIONAL INGREDIENTS

12 (½-inch-thick) baguette slices

¼ cup cream cheese, softened

½ cup crumbled blue cheese

1 tablespoon chopped fresh chives, plus more for garnish

2 small plum tomatoes, thinly sliced

⟢ VARIATION ⟣

Not a blue cheese fan? Try this with goat cheese instead. Not a goat cheese fan? Try it with feta.

¼ cup Sriracha chili sauce

¼ cup packed light brown sugar

10 thick-cut bacon slices, each cut into
    4 pieces

1½ tablespoons toasted sesame seeds

1½ tablespoons black sesame seeds

Bacon candy. Those two words are not often used together, and in fact you may not have ever associated them. But now, having considered the possibilities, you're probably like me and thinking this combination sounds amazing. It is! The brown sugar, Sriracha, and bacon remind me of a party where I introduce three of my favorite people to each other and watch them become best friends. Taste-wise, this is an irresistible collaboration of sweet, spicy, and savory. It's one of my favorite appetizers to make for a cocktail party. They always go fast. These bacon bites also package well, so I've made them in advance and given them to people as yummy gifts.

Brown Sugar Sriracha Bacon Bites
SERVES **10**   HANDS-ON **10 MINUTES**   TOTAL **1 HOUR**

1 Preheat the oven to 325°F. Stir together the Sriracha and brown sugar in a medium bowl; add the bacon pieces, and toss to coat. Set aside.

2 Line a large rimmed baking sheet with aluminum foil; place a wire rack over the foil. Spray the rack liberally with cooking spray. Place the bacon pieces in a single layer on the rack.

3 Bake the bacon until almost crisp, about 45 minutes. During the last 5 minutes, sprinkle the bacon evenly with the toasted sesame seeds and black sesame seeds.

4 Remove from the oven, and cool for 5 to 8 minutes, moving the bacon pieces slightly on the rack every 2 minutes to prevent sticking. (The bacon will crisp more as it cools.)

AROUND THE TABLE

Whether it's just Tom and myself or our entire family, dinner is a special time for me. It's more about coming together to share conversation than it is about consuming a meal. The best way to get everyone to the table on time is to let the aroma of a delicious meal serve as its own calling card. That's how it was when I was a child: Dinnertime meant family time—kids around the table, my dad at the head, but my mother in charge.

We might be playing outside and as it started to get dark, we would catch a savory hint in the air of something delicious happening in our kitchen. It was a subtle tap on the shoulder, a gentle whisper in our ear. *Dinnertime.* And we would run home, knowing Mom would be just about ready for everyone to sit down. In Delaware, where we lived until I was 9, we ate around a large dining room table. After moving to California, we gathered in our larger kitchen, reserving the dining room for special occasions.

For meals with both family and company, my mom relied on a greatest hits lineup of roasted chicken, lasagna, spaghetti and meatballs, and risotto, though she also branched out enough to fill a box with 3x5 recipe cards. In terms of quality and consistency, she set a high bar, as did so many women of her generation who saw their job as staying home to cook, clean the house, and raise the family. When I set out on my own, I worked full time and had a lot of catching up to do in the kitchen. During my first marriage, my husband had very little interest in food. His music provided all the nourishment he needed. Today, my life is different. Tom loves food, and also loves to cook. We schedule date nights in the kitchen where we share chef duties. We put some music on, open a bottle of wine—my idea of the perfect date.

I have carefully engineered the selections in this chapter to get everyone in your family to the dinner table, too. The recipes I've chosen represent an array of options from quick and easy weeknight meals to soups and pastas and time-savers you make in a slow cooker, along with favorites of mine for special occasions. As you'll see from the marinated flatiron steak, my mom's risotto, a quick and simple rotisserie chicken gumbo (there will be a chilly night and you'll thank me), my Aunt Norma's sauerkraut and pork, and a spicy arrabiata

penne that is literally a three-times-a-week go-to in my house, I've shared dishes that are practical and personal. I took dozens of recipe cards from my own files, arranged them across my dining room table, and gradually narrowed them down to be of the most use to you across a variety of needs.

These dishes represent many years of experience in the kitchen. My evolution from a girl who thought her first slice of New York pizza was the ultimate in fine dining to being able to confidently whip up a mouth-watering pasta alla vognole on short notice has taken decades. And I'm still learning. It takes time to acquire the experience of my mom and the women of her generation. That sort of intuitive knowledge and expertise does not happen overnight. However, that's the beauty of the recipes in this chapter. They enable us to take advantage of the past and put our own stamp on the present.

Now, what's for dinner?

5 tablespoons mixed peppercorns

3 tablespoons Dijon mustard

3 tablespoons unsalted butter, softened

¼ cup chopped fresh flat-leaf parsley

2½ pounds center-cut beef tenderloin, trimmed and tied if uneven

1 tablespoon kosher salt

Savory Horseradish Panna Cotta (recipe follows)

Freshly ground black pepper

MAKE AHEAD

The beef can be prepared up through Step 1, covered, and refrigerated for up to a day in advance. The panna cottas can be made and stored in the fridge, covered with plastic wrap, for up to 2 days in advance.

♦ TRICK TECHNIQUE ♦

The wire rack is important here as it lets the beef cook evenly.

This is one of my husband's specialties, and I've stolen it from him. Beef tenderloin is a classy cut of meat that I serve for company or holidays. Since it has very little fat, you have to supply the flavor, which is where the pepper and seasoning come in. Otherwise, the oven does all the hard work. I portion into half- to three-quarter-inch-thick slices and serve with either sautéed asparagus, spinach, or haricots verts. Also, a dollop of creamy horseradish panna cotta supplies an extra bit of flair that makes each bite heavenly. Tom made this for my parents on our first Christmas together. He was incredibly nervous. But as long as it's not overcooked, the tenderloin is mistake-proof, as evidenced by my parents' reaction. They talked about that dinner for years afterward. "Do you remember Tom's incredible beef tenderloin?" "Tom, if you make that again, you must have us over." He did make it again, and they enjoyed it many more times, as will you.

Peppered Beef Tenderloin

SERVES **6**   HANDS-ON **20 MINUTES**   TOTAL **1 HOUR, 5 MINUTES**

1   Preheat the oven to 450°F. Coarsely grind the peppercorns in a spice grinder or coffee grinder. Combine the mustard, butter, and 2 tablespoons of the parsley in a small bowl, stirring until blended. Rub the mustard mixture over the beef. Sprinkle the beef with the salt and ground peppercorns.

2   Place the beef on a wire rack in a rimmed baking sheet. Bake the beef until a meat thermometer inserted in the center registers 120°F, about 30 minutes. Increase the oven temperature to broil, and broil until browned and a meat thermometer inserted in the center registers 145°F (medium-rare) or to desired degree of doneness, about 3 minutes. Remove from the oven, and let rest about 10 minutes. Transfer the beef to a cutting board, and sprinkle with the remaining 2 tablespoons parsley. Serve with the Savory Horseradish Panna Cotta, sprinkling with black pepper.

Savory Horseradish Panna Cotta

SERVES **6**   HANDS-ON **10 MINUTES**   TOTAL **4 HOURS, 10 MINUTES**

1 Coat 6 (4-ounce) ramekins with cooking spray. Stir together the sour cream, mustard, horseradish, and salt in a small bowl. Heat the half-and-half in a small saucepan over medium-high until just simmering.

2 Meanwhile, place the gelatin in a large bowl. Add the 3 tablespoons warm water, and stir until the gelatin is completely dissolved. Gradually add the warm half-and-half to the gelatin mixture, whisking constantly. Add the sour cream mixture, whisking gently until thoroughly combined. Pour the mixture into the prepared ramekins, and refrigerate until set, at least 4 hours.

3 Run a thin knife along the edge of each ramekin, and invert the panna cottas onto the plates. Sprinkle with the chives, and serve immediately.

1 cup sour cream

3 tablespoons Dijon mustard

2 tablespoons prepared horseradish

1 teaspoon kosher salt

1¾ cups half-and-half

2 teaspoons unflavored gelatin

3 tablespoons warm water

2 tablespoons thinly sliced fresh chives

ROASTED BEETS
WITH HERBS
PG 205

I don't believe a steak always has to be expensive to be flavorful, and that's the crux of my support for the often overlooked flatiron steak. It's similar to flank steak and you could substitute that here if you want, but I recommend giving the less-expensive cut a try. My trick is to marinate early, letting it bathe in the juices for at least two hours and soak up the intense flavors of the garlic, soy sauce, rosemary, mustard, and vinegar. If this sounds like an excuse to make your mouth tingle with anticipation, it is. Then, I alternate between searing in a pan atop the stove or broiling in the oven and serving with grilled vegetables and roasted potatoes. Leftovers are great for sandwiches (even a decadent French dip with melted cheese) or a great steak salad with fresh tomatoes.

California Marinated Flatiron Steaks

SERVES **8**   HANDS-ON **15 MINUTES**   TOTAL **2 HOURS, 30 MINUTES**

1 Heat ¼ cup of the olive oil in a small saucepan over medium. Add the garlic; cook, stirring often, until golden, about 30 seconds. Stir in the rosemary and soy sauce. Remove the pan from the heat; add the vinegar, sherry, and mustard. Cool 15 minutes.

2 Place the steaks in a large ziplock plastic bag; pour the marinade over the steaks. Seal the bag, and turn to coat. Chill 2 hours. Remove the steaks from the bag; discard the marinade.

3 Heat a grill pan over medium-high. Brush the grill pan with 1 tablespoon of the oil. Add 1 steak to the pan; cook until a meat thermometer inserted in the thickest portion registers 145°F (medium-rare) or to the desired degree of doneness, 4 to 5 minutes per side. Repeat the procedure with the remaining oil and steak. Let the steaks rest 5 minutes; cut the steaks diagonally across the grain into thin slices.

6 tablespoons olive oil

4 garlic cloves, smashed

1 teaspoon chopped fresh rosemary

2 teaspoons soy sauce

¼ cup red wine vinegar

¼ cup dry sherry

½ teaspoon dry mustard

2 (1-pound) flatiron steaks

1 (1½- to 2-pound) bone-in rib-eye steak (about 1½ inches thick)

1½ tablespoons canola oil

1½ teaspoons flaky sea salt

1 teaspoon black pepper

⅓ cup instant espresso granules

2 teaspoons ancho chili powder

1 tablespoon salted butter

My husband came up with this recipe, and if I hadn't already married him, it would've been love at first bite. The idea was born one night when we were thinking about a new way to season our steak. Tom had an aha moment when he looked in the cabinet where we keep our seasonings and found a jar of instant espresso, which is always there for when I make brownies. He mixed it with some ancho chili powder, and salt and pepper, then smashed the rub into both sides of the steak and let it sit for about 30 minutes, until all that espresso, all that chili, and all that salt and pepper turns from rub to liquid. Then you get your cast-iron skillet super hot—Tom puts it in the oven at 450°F to get it to the place where he feels it's ready—add vegetable oil and drop the steak in, cooking on high until a firm crust forms on both sides. We typically split one big ribeye. When we tried this the first time, we had no idea how it would turn out. But I'm happy to report it was beyond successful. Great crust, perfectly medium-rare interior, and deep, delicious flavor. This is probably the best steak I have eaten in my entire life.

Tom's Espresso Rib-Eye

SERVES **2**   HANDS-ON **15 MINUTES**   TOTAL **55 MINUTES**

1 Preheat the oven to 450°F. Rub both sides of the steak with ½ tablespoon of the oil, and sprinkle with the salt and pepper. Stir together the espresso granules and the ancho chili powder. Rub both sides of the steak with the espresso mixture, pressing to adhere. Let stand at room temperature about 30 minutes.

2 Place a large cast-iron skillet in the preheated oven until hot, about 10 minutes.

3 Remove the hot skillet from the oven; add the remaining 1 tablespoon oil, and place over high on the stovetop. Add the steak to the skillet, and cook, undisturbed, until a crust has formed, 2½ to 3 minutes. Flip the steak and cook, undisturbed, for 2½ to 3 minutes. Using tongs, hold the steak upright to brown the edges, and cook, turning occasionally, until the edges are browned, about 6 minutes.

4 Return the skillet to the preheated oven, and bake until a meat thermometer inserted in the thickest portion registers 145°F, 6 to 8 minutes for medium-rare, or to the desired degree of doneness. Remove the steak from the skillet; top with the butter, and let rest about 10 minutes before slicing.

Don't laugh. This dish might give you more insight into my culinary history than almost anything else. It's a throwback to my childhood and it speaks directly to my more-than-occasional desire for quickness and efficiency, in that I love a good casserole or one-skillet dish. No fuss, no muss, easy cleanup, and get-right-to-it dinner. I made this for Wolfie and his friends when they came home after soccer or Little League practice. I can still picture everyone at the kitchen table, doing homework, while I simmered the beef in the mélange of spices and added macaroni, cheese, and breadcrumbs, and then announced to a sea of smiling faces, "Dinner's ready." Years later, I whipped out this dish when Tom's kids entered the picture and everyone came home from college during breaks. We all know the store-bought mix; this homemade version is even better than the classic, I promise.

Hamburger Helpa

SERVES **4**   HANDS-ON **10 MINUTES**   TOTAL **35 MINUTES**

1 Melt the butter in a large cast-iron skillet over medium-high. Add the beef, black pepper, and ½ teaspoon of the salt; cook, stirring to crumble, until browned, about 5 minutes.

2 Preheat the broiler with the oven rack 3 to 4 inches from the heat. Reduce the stovetop heat to medium, and stir in the macaroni. Add the milk, warm water, mustard, paprika, garlic powder, cayenne pepper, and remaining ½ teaspoon salt. Bring to a low simmer; cover, reduce the heat to low, and cook, stirring occasionally, until the macaroni is tender, about 12 minutes. Add the cheeses, and cook, stirring constantly, until the cheeses melt. Stir in the chives. Sprinkle the panko over the macaroni mixture. Broil until the panko is golden brown, 1 to 2 minutes. Garnish with the scallion, and serve immediately.

2 tablespoons unsalted butter

1 pound ground 90% lean beef

¼ teaspoon black pepper

1 teaspoon kosher salt

8 ounces uncooked elbow macaroni

2 cups whole milk

1¼ cups warm water

¼ teaspoon dry mustard

¼ teaspoon paprika

¼ teaspoon garlic powder

⅛ teaspoon cayenne pepper

1½ cups shredded sharp Cheddar cheese

½ cup chopped American cheese

2 tablespoons thinly sliced fresh chives

¼ cup panko (Japanese-style breadcrumbs)

1 scallion, green part sliced

VARIATION

Add some slices of jalapeño for extra kick.

¾ cup dry red wine

3 tablespoons olive oil

2 tablespoons balsamic vinegar

1 tablespoon coarse ground mustard

2 teaspoons chopped fresh thyme, plus more for garnish

1 teaspoon chopped fresh garlic

2 teaspoons kosher salt

½ teaspoon black pepper

8 (¾-inch-thick) lamb rib chops, trimmed

When my son, Wolfie, was little and we first moved out on our own, I wanted to make him special dinners every night, which, in a Monday through Friday reality, translated to lamb chops and asparagus or lamb chops and broccoli, or lamb chops and cauliflower and . . . you get the picture. The first few times he loved them, and I thought, great, I have a go-to meal. But I probably went to that meal a little too often. Eventually, he came in, did his homework or played his game, and said, "Mom, what are we having for dinner—and please don't say lamb chops." Admittedly, I get stuck on a favorite and have it night after night, but in this case, I didn't have the repertoire or confidence to branch out much. Eventually, I stretched out the time between servings until he asked for them again, and today we consider this a family classic. The marinade takes minutes to make. Then the chops sit in this bath of vinegar and seasonings for a few hours, until you're ready to throw them on the grill. These are clean and straightforward, with added support from roasted potatoes and an arugula salad. My advice is to use the highest quality chop you can find, since this dish is all about the flavor of the meat. Oh, if you have an unfinished bottle of red wine sitting around for a few days, leave it with your vinegars and use it in the marinade. You will enjoy, I have no doubt.

Marinated Lamb Chops

SERVES **8**   HANDS-ON **15 MINUTES**   TOTAL **2 HOURS, 15 MINUTES**

1 Whisk together the wine, oil, vinegar, mustard, thyme, garlic, 1 teaspoon of the salt, and ¼ teaspoon of the pepper. Place the lamb chops in a shallow baking dish or ziplock bag; pour the marinade over the lamb chops. Cover, or seal, and chill 2 to 4 hours, turning the lamb chops once.

2 Preheat the grill to medium-high (about 450°F). Remove the lamb chops from the marinade; discard the marinade. Sprinkle the lamb chops evenly with the remaining 1 teaspoon salt and ¼ teaspoon pepper. Place the lamb chops on the oiled grates; grill, uncovered, until seared on each side or to the desired degree of doneness, 3 to 4 minutes per side. Garnish with chopped thyme and serve immediately.

RISSOLE
POTATOES
PG 211

Chicken is one of the heroes of the dinner table, and by that I mean it's a consistent and reliable pleaser when I don't know what else to make. I suppose that's the reason people frequently compare dishes to the taste of chicken; it's familiar and extremely palatable. My special focus when cooking any variation of chicken is to not let it get dry, and this lemon-wine sauce is one of the best ways to accomplish that. The chicken comes out very crispy and with a hint of garlic flavor from the infused oil—a tangy and flavorful way to turn a basic chicken into a more sophisticated treat. Plus, the lemon-wine sauce goes wonderfully with rice, broccoli, potatoes, or green beans. Since this dish goes with a variety of side dishes and is family-friendly, you can file it under "always dependable."

Chicken with Lemon-Wine Sauce

SERVES **6**   HANDS-ON **26 MINUTES**   TOTAL **46 MINUTES**

1 Preheat the oven to 350°F. Place the chicken breasts between 2 pieces of plastic wrap, and flatten to ½-inch thickness, using a small heavy skillet or the flat side of a meat mallet. Place the egg in a shallow dish. Place the breadcrumbs in another shallow dish. Dip the chicken, 1 piece at a time, in the egg, shaking off the excess. Dredge in the breadcrumbs.

2 Heat 3 tablespoons of the oil in a large skillet over medium. Add the garlic to the skillet; cook until lightly browned, about 2 minutes. Remove the garlic from the skillet using a slotted spoon; discard the garlic.

3 Cook half of the chicken in the hot oil until golden brown, 2 to 3 minutes per side. Place the chicken on a baking sheet. Add the remaining 1 tablespoon oil to the skillet. Cook the remaining half of the chicken until golden brown, 2 to 3 minutes per side; transfer to the baking sheet. Bake the chicken until cooked through, 15 to 20 minutes.

4 Meanwhile, dissolve the bouillon cubes in the ¾ cup boiling water. Add the bouillon broth, wine, and lemon juice to the drippings in the skillet; cook over medium-high until reduced to about ¾ cup, about 8 minutes.

5 Remove the chicken from the oven, and transfer to a serving platter. Pour the sauce over the chicken, and sprinkle with the pecorino romano and thyme.

6 (6-ounce) boneless, skinless chicken breasts

2 large eggs, lightly beaten

1 cup Italian-seasoned breadcrumbs

¼ cup olive oil

2 large garlic cloves, halved

2 chicken-flavored bouillon cubes

¾ cup boiling water

¾ cup dry white wine

3 tablespoons fresh lemon juice (from 2 lemons)

⅓ cup shaved fresh pecorino romano cheese

1 teaspoon fresh thyme leaves

⌐ VARIATION ⌐

For a speedier dish, use chicken cutlets and cook entirely in the skillet for 3 to 4 minutes per side.

½ cup unsalted butter

1 medium russet potato, peeled and diced

¾ cup chopped yellow onion

½ cup sliced carrot

1 small red bell pepper, chopped

1½ cups sliced cremini mushrooms

2 teaspoons minced fresh garlic

¼ teaspoon crushed red pepper

1¼ teaspoons kosher salt

¾ teaspoon black pepper

1 (8-ounce) package microwave-in-bag haricots verts

3 cups shredded boneless, skinless rotisserie chicken (from 1 rotisserie chicken)

½ cup frozen green peas, thawed

½ (14.1-ounce) package refrigerated piecrusts (1 piecrust)

2½ tablespoons all-purpose flour

1½ cups chicken stock

½ cup heavy cream

1 tablespoon hot sauce, plus more for serving (optional)

1 large egg, lightly beaten

Chopped fresh flat-leaf parsley

>∘ VARIATION ∘<

You can easily substitute thawed frozen green beans for the French haricots verts in this homey dish.

When I was newly living on my own at 18 years old, I stocked my refrigerator with Swanson chicken potpies. I learned that from my mom, who also made her own chicken potpie when time allowed, which was always a treat. I would marvel at the way she mixed the ingredients in her large cast-iron skillet and covered it with pie crust, all without looking at a recipe, and then magically the potpie appeared on the table, feeding the entire family. It's been a long time since then, but the memory of those pies, both the frozen and homemade, are still fresh—as is the taste of a fork heaped with chicken, vegetables, gravy, and pie dough.

Jump ahead to several years ago. I got a taste for chicken potpie and wanted to make one on my own. The big revelation was how easy it was, not to mention the satisfaction I got using up the extra carrots, potatoes, onions, and peas in my vegetable drawer. This is basically a delicious chicken stew topped with a nice, crispy crust. Rich, creamy, and delicious, it's comfort food at its best and a great choice on a cool fall or winter evening.

Chicken Potpie

SERVES **6**　HANDS-ON **55 MINUTES**　TOTAL **1 HOUR, 25 MINUTES**

1 Preheat the oven to 375°F. Melt 2 tablespoons of the butter in a 10-inch cast-iron skillet over medium-high. Add the potato, onion, and carrot; cook, stirring occasionally, 6 minutes. Add the bell pepper, mushrooms, garlic, crushed red pepper, ½ teaspoon of the salt, and ¼ teaspoon of the black pepper. Reduce the heat to medium, and cook, stirring often, until the potatoes are almost tender, about 8 minutes.

2 Cook the haricots verts according to the package directions. Cool slightly, and cut into 1-inch pieces. Add the haricots verts, chicken, and peas to the potato mixture. Remove from the heat, and set aside.

3 Remove the piecrust from the refrigerator, and let stand 15 minutes. Meanwhile, melt the remaining 6 tablespoons butter in a large saucepan over medium. Whisk in the flour, and cook, whisking constantly, 1 minute. Gradually whisk in the chicken stock, and cook, whisking constantly, until the mixture thickens, about 10 minutes. Whisk in the heavy cream, hot sauce, and the remaining ¾ teaspoon salt and ½ teaspoon black pepper. Pour the cream sauce over the chicken mixture in the skillet, and stir gently to combine.

4 Unroll the piecrust, and fit over the filling, fluting around the edges, if desired. Brush the crust lightly with the beaten egg, and cut 4 small slits for the steam to escape. Bake until the filling is bubbly and the crust is golden brown, about 30 minutes. Let stand about 10 minutes before serving. Garnish with the chopped parsley, and serve with the hot sauce, if desired.

This is one of my mom's recipes that she made for my brothers and me on regular weeknight dinners. Not until recently did I consider how advanced her skills were to make these for our entire family. She was part gourmet chef and part short order cook, and versatile enough to experiment with little French pancakes. I've updated it slightly, with a little more intense seasoning, without monkeying with the traditional thrill of tasting chicken in a cream sauce laced with sherry. Time-consuming but worth every minute it takes to melt the butter, whisk the cream, and fold your crêpes, this dish indulges any comfort food mood. Make this when you want to seriously impress family or friends with a rich, creamy, and delicious meal. I only make this on a special occasion when everyone is hanging out in the kitchen, laughing, listening to music, and perhaps sharing in the process of making a romaine salad for the side.

Chicken à la King Crêpes

SERVES **5**   HANDS-ON **1 HOUR, 26 MINUTES**
TOTAL **2 HOURS, 26 MINUTES**

1   Process the milk, eggs, 1 cup of the flour, 3 tablespoons of the melted butter, and ¾ teaspoon of the salt in a blender until smooth. Cover and chill for 1 hour.

2   Meanwhile, heat 2 tablespoons of the butter in a large skillet over medium-high. Add the onion and mushrooms; cook, stirring occasionally, until just tender, about 8 minutes. Add the bell pepper, black pepper, and remaining ½ teaspoon salt; cook, stirring occasionally, until the vegetables are tender, about 8 minutes. Add the sherry, and cook until the liquid is nearly evaporated, about 3 minutes. Transfer to a bowl, and set aside. Wipe the skillet clean with paper towels.

3   Heat the remaining 4 tablespoons of butter in the skillet over medium. Whisk in the remaining ¼ cup flour, and cook, whisking constantly, until lightly browned, about 1 minute. Gradually whisk in the broth; cook, whisking often, until the sauce is thickened, about 5 minutes. Whisk in the heavy cream, and cook, whisking often, about 1 minute. Reduce the heat to low; stir in the vegetable mixture, chicken, cayenne pepper, and 2 tablespoons of the parsley. Cover and keep warm.

4   Stir the chives and remaining 2 tablespoons parsley into the chilled batter. Heat a 10-inch nonstick skillet over medium-low. Brush the skillet lightly with about ½ tablespoon of the melted butter; pour about ¼ cup of the batter into the skillet. Quickly tilt the skillet in all directions so the batter covers the bottom of the pan. Cook until the crêpe is almost set and can be shaken loose, 1 to 2 minutes. Turn the crêpe; cook about 30 seconds. Remove from the skillet; place about ¼ cup of the vegetable mixture on the crêpe, and fold the crêpe into quarters. Repeat the procedure with the remaining melted butter, crêpe batter, and vegetable mixture.

1 cup whole milk

4 large eggs

1¼ cups all-purpose flour

6 tablespoons unsalted butter, melted

1¼ teaspoons kosher salt

6 tablespoons unsalted butter

1½ cups chopped yellow onion

1 (8-ounce) package sliced button mushrooms

1 cup chopped red bell pepper

¼ teaspoon black pepper

¼ cup dry sherry

1¾ cups chicken broth

¼ cup heavy cream

4 cups shredded rotisserie chicken (from 1 large rotisserie chicken)

¼ teaspoon cayenne pepper

¼ cup chopped fresh flat-leaf parsley

2 tablespoons chopped fresh chives

MAKE AHEAD

The batter can be made up to 1 day in advance and refrigerated—or use store-bought crêpes.

SPICY BBQ SAUCE

1 tablespoon vegetable oil

1 small onion, chopped

2 garlic cloves, finely chopped

1 cup ketchup

½ cup water

½ cup apple cider vinegar

½ cup molasses

1 tablespoon Worcestershire sauce

2 canned chipotle peppers in adobo sauce, seeded and minced (about 1 tablespoon)

1 teaspoon kosher salt

½ teaspoon ground allspice

¼ teaspoon ground cloves

BARBECUE CHICKEN

6 chicken leg quarters (about 2½ pounds)

2 teaspoons kosher salt

2 teaspoons black pepper

MAKE AHEAD

The BBQ sauce can be made up to 1 week ahead of time—it yields 2½ cups.

᏶ COOKING TIP ᏶

Remember to move the chicken around the grill to keep it tender, but not so much that the skin doesn't crisp slightly.

For me, this is a summer-only staple, and the reason is the BBQ sauce: It's irresistible. I always make extra portions for dipping. Another reason this barbecue chicken is a warm-weather dish? Afterwards, everyone can jump in the pool and rinse off the sticky remnants of that finger lickin' deliciousness. For reference, this is Kentucky masterpiece-style BBQ, clove-forward and aromatic, and on the sweet side thanks to the chemistry that happens between the apple cider vinegar, molasses, ketchup, chipotle peppers, cloves, and other seasonings. I made a version of this on my show—Tom and I double-booked friends for dinner and I pulled this together, along with baked beans and a lemon-basil granita, for what turned out to be a backyard feast. As far as I'm concerned, this is the best barbecue chicken I've had. Suddenly I'm wishing I made it more often. Keep in mind, the secret to this is the sauce. It's all about the sauce.

Barbecue Chicken with Spicy BBQ Sauce

SERVES **6**   HANDS-ON **45 MINUTES**   TOTAL **1 HOUR, 15 MINUTES**

1   Make the Spicy BBQ Sauce: Heat the oil in a saucepan over medium-high. Add the onion; cook, stirring occasionally, until softened, about 5 minutes. Add the garlic; cook, stirring constantly, until the garlic is golden, about 30 seconds. Add the ketchup, water, vinegar, molasses, Worcestershire sauce, chipotle peppers, salt, allspice, and cloves; bring to a boil. Reduce the heat to medium-low, and simmer, stirring occasionally, until thickened, 13 to 15 minutes. Transfer the mixture to a blender. Remove the center piece of the blender lid (to allow steam to escape); secure the lid on the blender, and place a clean towel over the opening in the lid. Process until smooth. Cover and refrigerate until ready to serve.

2   Make the Barbecue Chicken: Preheat the grill to high (450°F to 550°F). Reserve ¾ cup of the Spicy BBQ Sauce for serving.

3   Sprinkle the chicken with the salt and black pepper. Reduce the grill heat to medium (350°F to 450°F). Place the chicken, skin side down, on the lightly oiled grates; grill, uncovered, until well marked, 8 to 10 minutes. Reduce the grill heat to low (250°F to 350°F); cover and grill until a meat thermometer inserted in the thickest portion of the thigh registers 175°F, 35 to 40 minutes, basting with the remaining 1¾ cups Spicy BBQ Sauce every 5 minutes. Do not baste during the last 5 minutes to prevent cross-contamination. Serve the chicken with the reserved ¾ cup Spicy BBQ Sauce.

MICROWAVE
POTATO CHIPS
PG 210

2 tablespoons olive oil

8 ounces smoked sausage, sliced

1 shallot, thinly sliced

2 garlic cloves, chopped

⅛ teaspoon crushed red pepper

1 cup dry white wine

½ cup coconut milk

1 tablespoon salted butter

⅛ teaspoon ground turmeric

⅛ teaspoon ground ginger

1 teaspoon kosher salt

¼ teaspoon black pepper

1 pound clams in shells, scrubbed

1 tablespoon fresh lime juice

3 lemon thyme or thyme sprigs

Spicy Garlic Bread (recipe follows)

I love clams, and this love affair of mine has been going on since I was a little girl with my nose pressed against the backseat window of my parents' car on family road trips. We lived in Delaware at the time, and somewhere along the Pennsylvania Turnpike there was a restaurant where we always stopped, and every time I ordered the steamers. It wasn't typical fare for a 7- or 8-year-old, but I spent the previous 11 months thinking about those clams and even more I thought about dipping fresh, hard-crusted bread into garlic-and-butter-flavored broth. More recently, this memory has been updated by my friend, acclaimed chef Ludo Lefebvre, who serves mussels at his tiny bistro Petite Trois in Hollywood with a creamier sauce that gets more delicious with each bite. So for this book, I took it as a challenge to develop my own version of steamed clams. I tinkered in the kitchen for a few days, carefully taking notes until I got the flavors exactly as I wanted. Be forewarned: The clams need to be cleaned, the sandy grit and residue from ocean dwelling removed, either by soaking in salty water or rinsing in a bowl. The spicy garlic bread is to taste, and I serve this with either a chilled white wine or a bottle of cold beer.

Steamed Clams with Spicy Garlic Bread
SERVES **2**   HANDS-ON **20 MINUTES**   TOTAL **20 MINUTES**

1 Heat the oil in a large skillet over medium. Add the sausage; cook, stirring often, until golden brown, about 5 minutes. Transfer the sausage to drain on paper towels, reserving the drippings in the skillet. Place the sausage in a large serving bowl.

2 Add the shallot to the skillet; cook, stirring often, until translucent and tender, 3 to 4 minutes. Stir in the garlic and crushed red pepper; cook for 1 minute. Add the wine, stirring and scraping to loosen the browned bits from the bottom of the skillet. Stir in the coconut milk, butter, turmeric, ginger, salt, and black pepper. Add the clams; cover the skillet, and let the mixture steam until the clams open, 6 to 7 minutes.

3 Transfer the clams to the bowl with the sausage. Stir the lime juice into the broth. Pour the broth over the clams and sausage. Remove the leaves from the thyme sprigs; discard the stems. Sprinkle the clam mixture with the lemon thyme leaves. Serve immediately with the Spicy Garlic Bread.

Spicy Garlic Bread

SERVES **4**   HAND-ON **5 MINUTES**   TOTAL **10 MINUTES**

1 Preheat the oven to 350°F. Cut the bread in half lengthwise through the top of the loaf, cutting to, but not through, the opposite side. Cut the bread crosswise at 1-inch intervals, cutting to, but not through, the opposite side.

2 Stir together the butter, garlic, crushed red pepper, and salt. Spread the butter mixture over the bread and between the slices.

3 Bake until golden brown, 5 to 7 minutes.

1 (12-ounce) French bread loaf

¼ cup unsalted butter, softened

3 garlic cloves, minced

¼ teaspoon crushed red pepper

Pinch of kosher salt

¼ cup salted butter, plus more for greasing dish

1 medium yellow onion, finely chopped

1 (8-ounce) package sliced cremini mushrooms

¾ teaspoon table salt

¼ cup all-purpose flour

2 cups whole milk

1 cup chicken broth

8 ounces uncooked medium pasta shells

1 (6.7-ounce) jar Italian tuna in olive oil, drained and flaked

2 tablespoons chopped fresh flat-leaf parsley, plus more for garnish

¼ teaspoon black pepper

1 cup shredded sharp white Cheddar cheese

1½ cups crumbled salt and vinegar potato chips

⌐ VARIATION ⌐

Depending on what you have on hand, you can also use canned tuna and egg noodles for a more traditional version of this casserole.

My relationship with the tuna noodle casserole dates back to my student days at Robert Frost Junior High School. I was enrolled in the mandatory "elective" Home Economics, otherwise known as cooking and sewing class for girls (while the guys were in shop or auto repair classes). In this relic from the 1950s, we were taught, among other things, to make tuna noodle casserole. The teacher set the ingredients on the classroom table: a can of tuna, a can of mushroom soup, a bag of egg noodles, cream, and a box of Corn Flakes for the top. She extolled the virtues of leftovers. I proudly made it for my family at home and remember it being fun and tasting pretty good, too. Those days inspired this variation with homemade béchamel (or white sauce), fresh cremini mushrooms, pasta shells versus egg noodles, and salt and vinegar potato chips (or any flavor you prefer) crumbled on top. My version is different enough to feel contemporary without sacrificing any ties to the sturdy original. This is an easy-to-prepare, single-dish meal long on comfort and convenience, and my Home Economics teacher was right: The leftovers are delish.

Tuna Noodle Casserole with Potato Chip Topping

SERVES **6**   HANDS-ON **50 MINUTES**   TOTAL **1 HOUR, 20 MINUTES**

1 Preheat the oven to 375°F. Grease a 2-quart baking dish with butter.

2 Melt ¼ cup butter in a large skillet over medium. Add the onion; cook, stirring occasionally, until slightly softened, about 5 minutes. Increase the heat to medium-high, and add the mushrooms and ¼ teaspoon of the salt. Cook, stirring occasionally, until the mushrooms are golden brown, 8 to 10 minutes. Sprinkle with the flour, and cook, stirring constantly, about 1 minute. Reduce the heat to medium. Gradually add the milk, stirring constantly; stir in the broth. Bring the mixture to a simmer, and cook, stirring constantly, until thickened, about 2 minutes.

3 Cook the pasta in salted water according to the package directions. Drain the pasta, and return to the saucepan. Add the mushroom mixture, tuna, and parsley; stir gently to combine. Sprinkle with the pepper and the remaining ½ teaspoon salt.

4 Transfer the pasta mixture to the prepared baking dish. Sprinkle with the cheese and crumbled potato chips. Bake until the top is golden brown and the edges are bubbly, about 25 minutes. Let stand 5 minutes before serving, sprinkled with more parsley.

Who doesn't like mac and cheese? I suppose it would be more meaningful to say that everyone likes mac and cheese, especially yours truly and my extended family. For that reason alone, I made it a point to develop a recipe for this staple that I've enjoyed since childhood. But my, how this dish's public image has changed! From a satisfying last-minute filler Mom could make for the kids to a culinary magic trick whereby noodles and cheese are transformed into savory, smile-inducing surprises for even the most discriminating foodies. Offhand, I recall seeing (and tasting) versions highlighting lobster and steak. I've seen a scoop of creamy cheesy goodness atop pulled pork sandwiches. And I've seen mac 'n' cheese fried into addictive little balls served as pass-around hors d'oeurves at fancy parties. I mean, nothing shows the evolution of this dish like people in tuxedos and formals gushing over mac 'n' cheese. My version is for grown-ups and sophisticated kids. The four cheeses make it uber cheesy and teem with flavor, and the crab, which is pretty easy to find in stores, elevates it to main-course level. Depending on who's at the dinner table, I occasionally leave out the crab and have a four-cheese version that even picky eaters devour. Served with a salad, I say, "Perfecto."

Four-Cheese Crab Mac 'n' Cheese

SERVES **6**   HANDS-ON **35 MINUTES**   TOTAL **1 HOUR**

1 Preheat the oven to 375°F. Lightly grease a 13- x 9-inch baking dish. Cook the pasta according to the package directions for al dente. Set aside.

2 Melt ¼ cup of the butter in a Dutch oven over medium. Whisk in the flour, and cook, whisking constantly, until smooth, about 2 minutes. Gradually whisk in the warm milk; increase the heat to medium-high, and cook, whisking constantly, until almost simmering, about 10 minutes. Stir in the hot sauce, salt, and pepper; cook, whisking often, until slightly thickened and bubbly, about 5 minutes. Remove from the heat.

3 Add the Cheddar, Gruyère, fontina, and 1 cup of the Parmesan; stir until the cheeses melt and the mixture is smooth.

4 Pour the cheese sauce over the hot cooked pasta in a large bowl; stir to coat. Gently stir the crabmeat into the pasta mixture. Pour the mixture into the prepared baking dish. Melt the remaining ¼ cup butter. Stir together the melted butter, panko, and remaining ¼ cup Parmesan; sprinkle over the pasta mixture. Bake until the top is golden brown and the edges are bubbly, about 25 minutes. Garnish with the scallions.

1 (1-pound) package cavatappi pasta

½ cup unsalted butter

¼ cup all-purpose flour

1 quart whole milk, warmed

1 tablespoon hot sauce

1 teaspoon kosher salt

½ teaspoon black pepper

2 cups shredded mild Cheddar cheese (about 8 ounces)

1 cup shredded Gruyère cheese

1 cup shredded fontina cheese

1¼ cups shredded Parmesan cheese

1 pound jumbo lump crabmeat, drained and picked to remove any bits of shell

1 cup panko (Japanese-style breadcrumbs)

⅓ cup sliced scallions

INGREDIENT NOTE
I recommend buying blocks of cheese and shredding it yourself; it just melts that much better!

- 1 (28-ounce) can diced tomatoes, undrained
- 3 cups water
- 1½ teaspoons kosher salt
- ¾ teaspoon black pepper
- 3 tablespoons olive oil
- 1 pound ground pork
- 1 cup chopped yellow onion
- 1 cup chopped celery
- 2 teaspoons chopped fresh garlic
- 1 cup uncooked Arborio rice
- ½ cup dry white wine
- 1 (5-ounce) package baby spinach
- ½ cup grated Parmesan cheese, plus shaved Parmesan cheese for serving

◦ VARIATION ◦

Feel free to substitute pork sausage if you so desire.

I think of this as an upscale, one-dish meal I can serve during the week. It's creamy, with al dente rice, as risotto should be, and the combination of spinach, tomatoes, and pork make this a hearty meal. But let me give you some background. My mom made risotto throughout my childhood and I thought it was the most delicious thing to ever rest on my tongue. If there was a meal I regarded as special, this was it. However, there was a catch. When she made her roasted chicken, she saved the neck, gizzards, and liver, and then always made risotto the next day, using those leftover chicken parts to kick up the flavor. I ate around them, pushing them all over my plate with an expression of disgust that never left my face until I put my plate in the sink for washing. I have, of course, eliminated these from my version, using ground pork instead. With crusty bread and a salad, this is a winner that can become, as it's been for me, a favorite family recipe. I'll just add one more note: Thanks, Mom.

Mom's Risotto (Sorta)

SERVES **4**   HANDS-ON **1 HOUR**   TOTAL **1 HOUR, 10 MINUTES**

1 Combine the tomatoes, water, 1 teaspoon of the salt, and ½ teaspoon of the pepper in a small saucepan. Cook over medium-low until thoroughly heated; keep warm.

2 Heat 1 tablespoon of the oil in a Dutch oven over medium. Add the pork, and cook, stirring to crumble, until browned, about 10 minutes. Transfer the pork to a plate lined with paper towels to drain; set aside. Discard the drippings.

3 Heat the remaining 2 tablespoons oil in the Dutch oven over medium. Add the onion, celery, and remaining ½ teaspoon salt and ¼ teaspoon pepper; cook, stirring occasionally, until the onion and celery are tender, about 10 minutes. Stir in the garlic, and cook 1 minute. Add the rice, and cook, stirring constantly, until the rice is lightly toasted, about 2 minutes. Stir in the wine, and cook until the liquid is nearly absorbed, about 2 minutes. Reduce the heat to medium-low, and add about 2 cups of the warm tomato mixture; cook, stirring occasionally, until the liquid is absorbed, about 4 minutes. Continue adding the tomato mixture, 1 cup at a time, waiting for the liquid to be absorbed after each addition, stirring occasionally, until the mixture is creamy and the rice is just tender, about 25 minutes. Remove from the heat.

4 Add the pork, spinach, and grated Parmesan; stir until the spinach wilts. Garnish with the shaved Parmesan.

If you haven't figured it out yet, my version of home cooking is all about family, both pleasing those at the table and drawing inspiration from those who came before me. The secret ingredient is always love, and so it is here. Aunt Norma was my father's youngest sister. When I was a little girl, she was always in the kitchen with my mom. The two of them worked and talked with an intuitive sync, and it was fun to watch them. These were women who really knew how to cook. My aunt gave this recipe to my mom, and though I don't recall her making it that often, I put my own stamp on this by adding fennel, which I love, and some additional seasoning. The apples melt into the vegetable mix and give it body and sweetness. This is a time-saver whether you use the slow cooker to make it in the morning or just reheat and serve over steamed rice.

Aunt Norma's Sauerkraut and Pork

SERVES **6**   HANDS-ON **30 MINUTES**   TOTAL **8 HOURS, 30 MINUTES**

1 Combine the sauerkraut, apple wedges, onion slices, fennel slices, water, vinegar, mustard, fennel seeds, brown sugar, ½ teaspoon of the salt, and ¼ teaspoon of the pepper in a 5-quart slow cooker.

2 Heat the oil in a large skillet over medium-high. Sprinkle the pork evenly with the remaining 1½ teaspoons salt and ½ teaspoon pepper. Add half of the pork ribs to the skillet; cook, turning occasionally, until browned on all sides, about 6 minutes. Repeat the process with the remaining pork ribs. Place the pork ribs on top of the sauerkraut mixture in the slow cooker. Cover and cook on LOW until the apples and pork are tender, about 8 hours. Remove the pork from the slow cooker, and shred into large pieces. Serve the pork over the sauerkraut mixture; garnish with the chopped parsley.

1 (16-ounce) package refrigerated sauerkraut, drained

3 small Granny Smith apples, peeled, cored, and cut into 1-inch wedges

1 large Vidalia or other sweet onion, thinly sliced

1 cup sliced fennel bulb

1 cup water

2 tablespoons apple cider vinegar

2 tablespoons spicy brown mustard

1 tablespoon fennel seeds

1 teaspoon light brown sugar

2 teaspoons kosher salt

¾ teaspoon black pepper

2 tablespoons olive oil

2 pounds boneless country-style pork ribs

2 tablespoons chopped fresh flat-leaf parsley

INGREDIENT NOTE
Sauerkraut is *so* good for your gut—all those wonderful natural probiotics.

MAKE AHEAD

This is a terrific dish to make over the weekend and refrigerate until you need a quick weeknight meal on the table—you can make it up to a week ahead.

1 tablespoon canola oil

2½ pounds ground sirloin

¾ cup chopped green bell pepper

½ cup chopped celery

1 small yellow onion, chopped

1 tablespoon chopped garlic

1 cup tomato sauce

½ cup lemon-lime soda

½ cup ketchup

2 tablespoons yellow mustard

1 tablespoon ground cumin

1 tablespoon Worcestershire sauce

1 teaspoon kosher salt

1 teaspoon dried oregano

½ teaspoon black pepper

3 tablespoons apple cider vinegar

8 hamburger buns

INGREDIENT NOTE

I know, you're wondering about that can of soda. It provides a subtle undercurrent of sweet and sour and fun-zone burst of flavor.

MAKE AHEAD

Another great dish that can be made up to 1 week ahead and quickly reheated during the week.

Sloppy Joes are one of the things my mom made when she was just too tired to cook that night. She threw in the store-bought Manwich and gave herself the time off. She also knew that we loved them, and I mean, we loved them. When we heard Sloppy Joes were on the menu, my brothers and I literally cheered. "Yay! Sloppy Joes!" I told this story to a producer on my show before making these on camera and wondered why us kids got so excited for these when my mom's amazing lasagna, spaghetti and meatballs, and risotto failed to elicit such excitement. My producer said, "It's because these taste great and hit that special happy spot in all of us." Anyway, this is still the time-saving shortcut my mom enjoyed. Just throw the ingredients in the slow cooker in the morning and you have Sloppy Joes by dinnertime. For a party or a treat, you can also prepare these as sliders. Served with fries, Tater Tots, potato salad, or chips, this will delight all the kids, as well as the kid still lurking inside all of us slow-to-grow-up adults.

Slow-Cooker Sloppy Joes

SERVES **8**   HANDS-ON **15 MINUTES**   TOTAL **4 HOURS, 15 MINUTES**

1 Heat the oil in a large Dutch oven over medium-high. Add the beef, and cook, stirring to crumble, until browned, about 8 minutes. Stir in the bell pepper, celery, onion, and garlic; cook, stirring occasionally, until the onion is translucent, about 6 minutes. Drain well.

2 Transfer the beef mixture to a 5-quart slow cooker. Stir in the tomato sauce, soda, ketchup, mustard, cumin, Worcestershire sauce, salt, oregano, black pepper, and 2 tablespoons of the vinegar. Cover and cook on HIGH until slightly thickened, about 4 hours, or on LOW about 8 hours. Stir in the remaining 1 tablespoon vinegar. Serve the beef mixture on the hamburger buns.

HOMEMADE BAKED
POTATO TOTS
PG 207

This is Chinese takeout at home. What I love about this, besides the fact that it's a favorite of mine, is that the slow cooker does all the work. When I have a long day on the set, I put everything in the slow cooker before I leave for work and then I have a ready-to-eat meal when I return at night. The chicken stays tender, and I can vary the seasoning to taste depending on whom I'm feeding that night, whether it's Tom and me, who enjoy more acute flavors, or less-adventurous house guests. The chicken can also be made ahead of time and reheated and served over a bed of white rice. With an egg roll, it's convenient and still satisfying when you feel like ordering in without picking up the phone.

Slow-Cooker Sweet-and-Sour Chicken

SERVES **4**   HANDS-ON **30 MINUTES**   TOTAL **4 HOURS**

1 Heat 1 tablespoon of the oil in a large skillet over medium-high. Add the chicken to the skillet, and cook until golden brown, 3 to 4 minutes per side. Place the chicken in a 4- to 5-quart slow cooker.

2 Heat remaining 1 tablespoon oil in the skillet. Add the bell peppers and onion; cook, stirring occasionally, until tender and lightly browned, about 6 minutes. Add the vegetables to the slow cooker.

3 Whisk together the vinegar, ketchup, soy sauce, cornstarch, and sugar. Pour the mixture over the chicken and vegetables in the slow cooker. Cover and cook on LOW until the chicken is tender and cooked through, 3 hours and 30 minutes to 4 hours. Serve the chicken mixture over the hot cooked rice topped with the scallions and sesame seeds.

2 tablespoons canola oil

8 (8-ounce) bone-in chicken thighs, skin removed

1 red bell pepper, cut into 1-inch pieces

1 green bell pepper, cut into 1-inch pieces

1 white onion, cut into 1-inch pieces

⅓ cup rice vinegar

¼ cup ketchup

3 tablespoons soy sauce

2 tablespoons cornstarch

2 teaspoons granulated sugar

3 cups hot cooked white rice

¼ cup sliced scallions

1 tablespoon sesame seeds, toasted

INGREDIENT NOTE
Chicken thighs have more flavor and are more forgiving during cooking, staying juicy.

4 cups jarred marinara sauce

12 ounces uncooked ziti pasta

1 medium zucchini, cut into ¾-inch pieces (about 2 cups)

1½ cups matchstick carrots

1½ cups ricotta cheese (about 12 ounces)

1 cup shredded mozzarella cheese

¾ cup finely shredded Parmesan cheese

1 (2-ounce) can sliced black olives, drained

½ cup water

3 cups roughly chopped baby spinach

¼ cup fresh basil leaves

◇ VARIATION ◇

Choose your favorite vegetables! Just keep in mind if they're tender leafy greens like the spinach, stir them in at the end.

I don't mean to turn this into a confessional, but this dish came together because I saw a jar of marinara sauce sitting on the kitchen counter. Hey, inspiration comes in all shapes, sizes, and forms. But this is a traditional baked ziti with creamy ricotta and mozzarella, salty parm, and tender pasta, all just so yummy together, plus the carrots and zucchini. On occasion when I'm really busy, I'll go to the grocery store and get vegetables already chopped, and throw everything into the slow cooker for a nice dinner later on. It's a shortcut on top of a shortcut. I'm gentle when folding in the spinach, as the pasta could start to fall apart if you do this with hurried, crushing blows. Tom and I both like this with a fresh Caesar salad, but any crisp, cold, and simple green salad will go well with this dish.

Slow-Cooker Pasta Bake

SERVES **4**   HANDS-ON **15 MINUTES**   TOTAL **1 HOUR, 45 MINUTES**

1 Lightly coat a 5-quart slow cooker with cooking spray. Add the marinara sauce, pasta, zucchini, carrots, ricotta, mozzarella, Parmesan, olives, and water; stir to combine. Cover and cook on LOW until the pasta is tender, about 1 hour and 30 minutes to 2 hours.

2 Gently fold in the spinach until wilted. Spoon into serving bowls, and top evenly with the basil.

One of my all-time favorite meals centers around tomatoes. I have several photos on my phone illustrating this point. One shows a fresh harvest of tomatoes from our garden; they're literally spilling out of bowls onto the kitchen counter. I think this was a message from our wonderful gardener, Carlos. The first year I planted tomato plants, the majority of them died. I went to Carlos, asking for help. I think he felt bad for me, and not only did he bring those plants back to life, he added more and somehow has them producing fruit well into the winter. Another photo shows my arrabiata sauce simmering on the stove, tomatoes quartered and afloat on a sea of luscious sauce full of spices. I swear I can smell the red pepper and garlic through my phone. Fresh tomatoes are a bonus, but obviously canned tomatoes provide the same classic taste. This is an easy dinner when I'm in a hurry, and with a green salad and a creamy dressing to balance the spice, along with fresh bread, you can rely on this as a Monday through Friday staple, as I do, or serve it for a casual Saturday night with friends.

Spicy Arrabiata Penne

SERVES **6**   HANDS-ON **5 MINUTES**   TOTAL **20 MINUTES**

1 Bring a large pot of salted water to a boil. Add the pasta, and cook according to the package directions; drain, reserving 1 cup of the cooking water.

2 Meanwhile, heat the oil in a large skillet over medium-high until shimmering. Add the garlic; cook, stirring often, until fragrant, 1 to 2 minutes. Add the tomatoes, salt, crushed red pepper, Italian seasoning, and black pepper. Bring to a boil, and cook 5 minutes. Remove from the heat, and stir in the ¼ cup chopped basil.

3 Stir the cooked pasta and reserved pasta water into the tomato mixture. Garnish with the Parmigiano-Reggiano and additional basil, if desired, and serve warm.

1 (1-pound) package uncooked penne rigate

¼ cup olive oil

3 garlic cloves, chopped

1 (26.46-ounce) package chopped tomatoes (such as Pomì)

1 teaspoon kosher salt

½ teaspoon crushed red pepper

½ teaspoon dried Italian seasoning

¼ teaspoon black pepper

¼ cup chopped fresh basil, plus more for garnish

Shaved fresh Parmigiano-Reggiano cheese, for garnish

COOKING TIP

It's important to generously salt your water. It adds flavor to your pasta. Don't rinse your pasta after cooking, and don't drain all the water; save some to flavor your sauce.

12 ounces uncooked bucatini pasta

3 cups roughly chopped baby spinach

½ cup mascarpone cheese

½ teaspoon lemon zest, plus 1 teaspoon fresh lemon juice (from 1 lemon)

½ teaspoon kosher salt

½ teaspoon crushed red pepper

½ teaspoon black pepper

1 cup shaved fresh pecorino romano cheese

◦ VARIATION ◦

Feel free to throw in strips of leftover chicken for a heartier meal.

I'm sure you saw the lemon mascarpone sauce in the title and thought *Valerie has gone too far this time*. But trust me on this one. When it comes to inventing new dinner dishes, Tom and I are most creative, fearless, and successful with pasta, and this dish provides ample evidence. The goal was to come up with something slightly different and out of the mainstream, without veering too far, and to keep it relatively simple, something anyone could make on short notice. So we looked around. We had baby spinach and tomatoes in our garden. We had lemons and limes on our trees. I love mascarpone and had recently made a lime mascarpone and arugula pasta. Ergo, we had a wonderful meal with almost everything but the pasta and mascarpone coming from our yard. Note the crushed red pepper that adds that little bit of heat that seems to wake up each bite for me, and sprinkling fresh pecorino romano cheese on top? Well that last step provides a subtle flourish of salty flavor that ties everything back to my roots. This dish is similar to the way our ancestors ate, a fresh farm-to-table, keep-it-simple-and-delicious-will-result approach.

Bucatini with Wilted Spinach and Lemon Mascarpone Sauce

SERVES **4**   HANDS-ON **18 MINUTES**   TOTAL **18 MINUTES**

1 Cook the pasta according to the package directions. Drain the pasta, reserving 1 cup of the cooking water. Return the pasta to the saucepan; add the spinach and ¼ cup of the reserved cooking water, tossing gently to wilt the spinach.

2 Combine the mascarpone, lemon zest, lemon juice, salt, crushed red pepper, and black pepper in a medium bowl. Add ½ cup of the reserved cooking water; whisk until smooth and creamy. Add the mascarpone sauce to the pasta mixture, and toss well. Thin with the remaining pasta water, if necessary. Top with the pecorino romano, and serve warm.

If you are looking to whip up a rich pasta awash in flavor, one that gives you the sense of being especially indulgent yet you want to avoid both cream sauce and lots of preparation—you have found the perfect recipe. One day when I found myself considering Tom's and my dinner plans, I looked in the fridge and found bacon, arugula, and fresh basil. I already had tomatoes in a bowl on the counter. And I thought, "Wait a minute. This is a BLT. What if I put it all together?" I did, and the result was a splendidly tender pasta with a lightly acidic tomato-wine sauce that went perfectly with the smoky bacon. With the peppery kick of the arugula, it really was a BLT. You don't want to overlook the basil, either. For the nuance of its sweetness, pluck it from your garden or pick it up that day at the grocery store. This serves very simply from a large bowl and is enjoyable year-round, especially with a glass of wine.

BLT Pasta

SERVES **4**   HANDS-ON **25 MINUTES**   TOTAL **35 MINUTES**

1 Bring the water and ¼ cup of the salt to a boil in a large saucepan over high. Hull the stems from the tomatoes. Cut a shallow "x" through the skin on the bottom of each tomato.

2 Place the tomatoes in the boiling water, and boil about 30 seconds. Using a slotted spoon, remove the tomatoes, and submerge in a bowl of ice water to stop the cooking process. Reserve the salted water in the saucepan.

3 When the tomatoes are cool enough to handle, peel back the skin using a paring knife. Cut the tomatoes in half lengthwise; squeeze out and discard the seeds. Chop the tomatoes into ½-inch pieces.

4 Place the bacon in a cold large skillet; cook over medium, stirring occasionally, until crisp, 10 to 13 minutes. Drain the bacon on a paper towel-lined plate. Reserve 2 tablespoons drippings in the skillet.

5 Add the onion to the hot drippings in the skillet; cook over medium, stirring occasionally, until soft and lightly golden, about 10 minutes. Add the wine; cook until the liquid is reduced by half, about 3 minutes. Add the chopped tomatoes, black pepper, crushed red pepper, and remaining ½ teaspoon salt to the skillet; cook, stirring occasionally, until the tomatoes begin to break down, about 5 minutes.

6 Return the reserved salted water in the saucepan to a boil; add the spaghetti, and cook until al dente, about 10 minutes. Drain the pasta, reserving 1 cup of the cooking water. Add the pasta and ¼ cup of the reserved cooking water to the tomato mixture in the skillet; toss to coat. Add more cooking water, if necessary, until the mixture reaches the desired consistency. Transfer to a large bowl; toss with arugula and half of the chopped bacon. Divide evenly among 4 serving bowls; top evenly with the basil, remaining chopped bacon, and Parmesan.

12 cups water

¼ cup plus ½ teaspoon kosher salt

2 pounds plum tomatoes (about 10 tomatoes)

6 thick-cut bacon slices, chopped

1 medium yellow onion, halved and thinly sliced

½ cup dry white wine

¼ teaspoon black pepper

⅛ teaspoon crushed red pepper

12 ounces uncooked spaghetti

4 cups fresh baby arugula

¼ cup chopped fresh basil

Grated fresh Parmesan cheese

⮞ VARIATION ⮜

This is easily adaptable to whatever you have on hand, like spinach and linguine instead of the arugula and spaghetti.

⮞ COOKING TIP ⮜

This is another time I like to sauté my bacon instead of using the oven. All those yummy hot bacon drippings.

4 small bell peppers

4 small beefsteak tomatoes

2 tablespoons extra-virgin olive oil

1 cup chopped yellow onion

½ cup finely chopped fennel bulb
(fronds reserved)

1 tablespoon chopped fresh oregano

1 teaspoon ground cumin

1 teaspoon kosher salt

½ teaspoon black pepper

3 garlic cloves, chopped

2 tablespoons water

1 (9-ounce) pouch microwavable
quinoa (about 1½ cups)

1 cup Castelvetrano olives, pitted
and halved

½ cup crumbled feta cheese

2 tablespoons roughly chopped fennel
fronds

¼ cup chopped fresh flat-leaf parsley

½ cup panko (Japanese-style
breadcrumbs)

2 tablespoons freshly shredded
Parmesan cheese

1 tablespoon salted butter, melted

For years, I made this with ground beef or turkey, but I took them out of the equation in order to have a go-to for my vegetarian friends. I love green bell peppers, but only because of my gumbo. (You must have green peppers in gumbo—at least I believe you do.) But for stuffed peppers, I prefer to use the red, yellow, or orange variety. They are sweeter than the under-ripened green, equally healthy as sources for vitamins A and C, and much prettier on the plate, especially when I think about dining al fresco on the patio on a warm summer night. Getting the stuffing mixture just right involves a number of steps, but once you have it down, which means eventually experimenting to your own taste, it's worthwhile. I also surround these with fresh vegetable sides, like string beans, broccoli, or cauliflower, and a good Caesar or garden salad.

Vegetarian Stuffed Peppers and Tomatoes

SERVES **4**   HANDS-ON **40 MINUTES**   TOTAL **40 MINUTES**

1 Preheat the oven to 400°F. Cut ½ inch from the top (stem end) of each bell pepper and tomato. Finely chop the tomato tops to measure 1 cup and reserve, discarding the tomato stems, if necessary. Discard the bell pepper tops. Scoop out and discard the pulp and seeds from the bell peppers and tomatoes.

2 Place the bell pepper shells, cut sides up, in a lightly greased 8-inch square baking dish. Drizzle with 1 tablespoon of the oil. Bake until the peppers begin to soften, about 10 minutes. Remove from the oven, and set aside. Increase the oven temperature to broil with the oven rack 5 inches from the heat.

3 Heat the remaining 1 tablespoon oil in a large skillet over medium. Add the onion, fennel bulb, oregano, cumin, ½ teaspoon of the salt, and ¼ teaspoon of the black pepper; cook, stirring occasionally, until the onion is translucent, about 8 minutes. Add the garlic, and cook, stirring often, until fragrant, about 1 minute. Add the water and reserved 1 cup chopped tomatoes to the skillet; cook, stirring often, 3 minutes. Remove from the heat; stir in the quinoa, olives, feta, fennel fronds, 2 tablespoons of the parsley, and ¼ teaspoon of the salt.

4 Stir together the panko, Parmesan, and remaining 2 tablespoons parsley in a small bowl. Add the melted butter, and stir to combine.

5 Add the tomato shells to the baking dish, alternating with the bell pepper shells. Sprinkle the cavities evenly with the remaining ¼ teaspoon salt and ¼ teaspoon black pepper. Divide the quinoa mixture evenly among the tomato and bell pepper shells. Top evenly with the panko mixture.

6 Broil until the panko mixture is golden brown, about 2 minutes.

I'm a fan of eggplant, which I was surprised many years ago to learn is actually a fruit, though closer to tomatoes and potatoes than anything I regard as fruity. However, it's near and dear to my heart for its sculptured beauty, regal purple color, and gratifying meatiness—or perhaps chewiness—that I periodically crave. When that craving strikes, it's for this roasted eggplant and pesto pasta. There is a medley of strong flavors here: the tomatoes, the salty and briny olives, and the eggplant itself. The pesto you make by processing the olive oil, almonds, capers, and garlic is causing my mouth to water right now. With the addition of the feta, this has a wonderful garden-fresh taste. It's a great choice for when you want a gratifying but light and healthy dinner. Serve with a salad or fresh sourdough bread and your favorite white or red wine.

Roasted Eggplant Pesto Pasta

SERVES **4**　HANDS-ON **15 MINUTES**　TOTAL **35 MINUTES**

1　Preheat the oven to 475°F. Toss the eggplant with the 2 tablespoons olive oil, salt, and pepper; spread on a rimmed baking sheet. Bake until the eggplant is slightly tender, about 20 minutes.

2　Add the tomatoes and olives to the baking sheet, and bake until the tomatoes begin to burst and the eggplant is tender, about 5 minutes.

3　Process the ½ cup olive oil, almonds, capers, and garlic in a blender until smooth. Add the basil, oregano, and parsley; process just until smooth. Stir in the lemon juice.

4　Cook the pasta in salted water according to the package directions; drain. Toss the hot cooked pasta with the roasted vegetables, pesto mixture, and feta. Sprinkle with the basil leaves and serve.

3 cups (1-inch) cubed unpeeled eggplant (from about 1 pound eggplant)

2 tablespoons olive oil

1 teaspoon kosher salt

½ teaspoon black pepper

1 cup halved cherry tomatoes

½ cup halved pitted kalamata olives

½ cup extra-virgin olive oil

¼ cup whole blanched almonds

1 tablespoon capers, drained

2 teaspoons chopped fresh garlic

½ cup firmly packed fresh basil leaves, plus more for garnish

¼ cup firmly packed fresh oregano leaves

¼ cup firmly packed fresh flat-leaf parsley leaves

½ tablespoon fresh lemon juice

1 (16-ounce) package rotini pasta

½ cup feta cheese, cut into cubes

⸎ COOKING TIP ⸎

You don't have to, but I like to sweat eggplant to release extra water: Slice the eggplant and lay slices on a wire rack. Sprinkle with salt and let stand for 30 minutes. Pat dry and go to Step 1.

¾ pound ground chicken

1 large egg white, lightly beaten

¼ teaspoon kosher salt

⅛ teaspoon black pepper

½ cup grated fresh pecorino romano cheese

3 tablespoons olive oil

1 cup chopped yellow onion

½ cup sliced carrot

¼ cup chopped celery

½ cup uncooked pearl couscous

1½ teaspoons chopped fresh garlic

1 teaspoon chopped fresh rosemary

6 cups chicken broth

¼ cup chopped fresh parsley

◇ VARIATION ◇

The pearl couscous may be switched for rice or ditalini pasta, but the pearls are true to the original.

◆ TRICK TECHNIQUE ◆

Don't have a cookie scoop? These mini meatballs can also be formed by using a piping bag or ziplock bag with a corner snipped off. Simply spoon the sticky chicken mixture into the bag and squeeze out ½-inch meatballs.

So many of my favorite dishes are connected to memories from years ago, if not decades ago, and this is one of them. My son always loved a good meatball soup, and when Wolfie was a little boy and I didn't feel like cooking, I opened a can of Progresso Chickarina soup. It's regarded by many as the greatest tasting soup ever sold in a can, right up there next to Campbell's classic tomato soup. Years ago the grocery stores in my neighborhood quit carrying the chickarina soup, which led me on a quest to make my own—and all I can say is thank goodness I set out on that journey. The meatballs are the key to my version; they're tiny and sticky and decidedly unlike those you'd make for spaghetti and meatballs or turkey meatball soup. They have a unique consistency, enabling them to cook differently in the chicken broth. They end up as tasty little puffs. And yes, this requires an investment in time, mostly to make the meatballs. But it's worth the wait. This is comfort food at its finest—a perfect call for lunch or dinner on the coldest day of the year. Or take it in a thermos on an outdoor adventure—a widemouthed thermos, of course.

Chickarina Soup

SERVES **4**   HANDS-ON **30 MINUTES**   TOTAL **1 HOUR**

1 Preheat the broiler with the oven rack 6 to 8 inches from the heat. Line a baking sheet with aluminum foil, and coat with cooking spray. Gently combine the chicken, egg white, salt, pepper, and half of the pecorino romano. Scoop the mixture into meatballs using a ½-inch cookie scoop, and place the meatballs on the prepared baking sheet. Broil until the meatballs are lightly browned, about 6 minutes.

2 Heat the oil in a large Dutch oven over medium-high. Add the onion, carrot, and celery; cook, stirring often, until the onion is tender, about 6 minutes. Add the couscous, garlic, and rosemary; cook, stirring often, until the couscous is lightly toasted, about 2 minutes. Stir in the chicken broth, and bring to a boil. Add the meatballs, and cook until the couscous is tender and the meatballs are cooked through, 15 to 20 minutes. Top with the parsley and remaining half of the pecorino romano.

I learned to love gumbo when my family moved to New Orleans, the holy center of the gumbo universe. Then my brother Patrick married a good Southern girl from Louisiana named Stacy, who taught me to make a traditional Creole gumbo, the thick kind with andouille sausage, turkey, okra, bacon drippings, and the works. We make it every year the day after Thanksgiving, and it takes all day. It's an annual family event: football, gumbo, family. But sometimes I want to make gumbo and it's not the day after Thanksgiving, and I don't have the time to spend the whole day making it. As a result, I came up with a version of my own, one that starts with picking up a rotisserie chicken at the grocery store. If I'm not distracted, I have gumbo within an hour and a half. Lightly spiced. Nutty. Meaty. Serve with crusty bread or over rice, and then enjoy with family and friends. This is a good gathering-type food, like for a Sunday football game. It makes everyone feel like a winner.

Quick Rotisserie Chicken Gumbo

SERVES **8**   HANDS-ON **30 MINUTES**   TOTAL **50 MINUTES**

1 Cook the sausages in a large nonstick skillet over medium until browned, about 8 minutes. Remove the sausages from the skillet, and drain on paper towels.

2 Heat the oil in a large Dutch oven over medium-high; gradually whisk in the flour, and cook, whisking constantly, until the flour is a deep caramel color, 7 to 10 minutes.

3 Reduce the heat to medium. Stir in the onion, bell pepper, celery, garlic, thyme, Creole seasoning, and cayenne pepper; cook, stirring constantly, about 5 minutes. Gradually stir in the broth; add the chicken, tomatoes, okra, Worcestershire sauce, and sausage.

4 Increase the heat to medium-high, and bring the mixture to a boil. Reduce the heat to low, and simmer, stirring occasionally, about 20 minutes. Serve the gumbo over the hot cooked rice topped with the scallions. Serve with the hot sauce, if desired.

½ pound andouille sausage, cut into ¼-inch-thick slices

½ pound Polska kielbasa sausage, cut into ¼-inch-thick slices

½ cup peanut oil

½ cup all-purpose flour

1 cup chopped yellow onion

1 cup chopped green bell pepper

1 cup chopped celery

2 garlic cloves, chopped

1½ teaspoons chopped fresh thyme

1½ teaspoons Creole seasoning

¼ teaspoon cayenne pepper

5 cups low-sodium chicken broth

4 cups shredded rotisserie deli chicken (from 1 large rotisserie chicken)

1 (14.5-ounce) can diced tomatoes, undrained

1½ cups frozen cut okra

2 teaspoons Worcestershire sauce

4 cups hot cooked white rice

¼ cup sliced scallions

Hot sauce (optional)

⊱ VARIATION ⊰

I suggest changing out sausage types to suit your taste and mood; take advantage of the variety available, for instance using Conecuh instead of kielbasa. The more often you make gumbo, the better you get at putting your own stamp on it.

⊱ COOKING TIP ⊰

You can grill the sausage to get that extra smoky flavor and beautiful grill char.

POSOLE
PG 182

LOBSTER BISQUE
PG 184

**SPICY KILLER
SHRIMP SOUP**
PG 183

½ medium red onion, cut crosswise into 1-inch-thick slices

½ pound tomatillos (about 5 medium tomatillos), husks removed

2 large poblano chiles

¼ teaspoon black pepper

¼ cup canola oil

2 teaspoons kosher salt

¼ cup all-purpose flour

1 tablespoon chili powder

2 pounds boneless pork shoulder (Boston butt), cut into ½-inch cubes

6 cups chicken broth

2 (28-ounce) cans white hominy, drained and rinsed

1 jalapeño chile, seeded and minced

1 teaspoon chopped fresh oregano

1 cup chopped fresh cilantro

2 tablespoons fresh lime juice

1 medium ripe avocado, diced

¼ cup sliced radishes

⊲ VARIATION ⊳

You can substitute skinless, boneless chicken breasts for the pork shoulder.

Though posole is a traditional Mexican soup dating back to the Aztecs in the 1500s, I'd never heard of it when Tom and I were offered a bowl in a restaurant several years ago. (To lessen my embarrassment of being culturally ignorant, I will add that Tom had not heard of this soup, either.) Wonderfully aromatic, it had sliced radishes on top and with my initial spoonful, I tasted something that I first thought was chickpeas but then quickly learned was hominy. Hominy is made from kernels of corn, or maize, that have been cooked and dried until they're swollen and chewy. Tom tasted the soup and was also blown away. He wanted the rest for himself, and we actually battled over who got to finish this little bowl of soup. More embarrassment. But it was that good and I was determined to come up with my own recipe. Which meant educating myself—one of the most fun parts of cooking: learning and experimenting. I found hominy in a nearby Mexican market. I varied the spices and chiles, and tried this with both pork and chicken rather than one or the other. I also learned this soup is often regarded as a stew, depending on its thickness. You can add more hominy to give the soup an even heartier body. Even with the meat, this soup, with its hint of lime, zing of jalapeño, and tangy broth, tastes fresh and clean. Tom and I still battle over who gets the last bowl.

Posole

SERVES **6 AS A MAIN DISH, 12 AS AN APPETIZER**
HANDS-ON **30 MINUTES** TOTAL **1 HOUR**

1 Preheat the broiler with the oven rack 5 inches from the heat. Separate the onion slices into rings. Toss together with the tomatillos, poblanos, black pepper, 1 tablespoon of the oil, and 1 teaspoon of the salt on a rimmed baking sheet. Broil, turning occasionally, until blistered and charred in spots, about 8 minutes. Set aside to cool completely, about 20 minutes.

2 Meanwhile, stir together the flour, chili powder, and remaining 1 teaspoon salt in a large bowl. Add the pork, and toss to coat.

3 Heat the remaining 3 tablespoons oil in a large Dutch oven over medium-high. Add the pork, and cook, stirring occasionally, until browned on all sides, about 10 minutes. Add 5 cups of the chicken broth and 1½ cans of the hominy; bring to a boil. Reduce the heat to medium-low, and simmer 15 minutes.

4 Meanwhile, peel and seed the poblanos. Process the poblanos, tomatillos, onion rings, jalapeño, oregano, ¾ cup of the cilantro, remaining 1 cup chicken broth, and ½ can hominy in a blender until smooth. Add the mixture to the pork mixture in the Dutch oven; cook 15 minutes. Remove from the heat, and stir in the lime juice. Garnish the servings evenly with the avocado, radishes, and remaining ¼ cup cilantro.

For years, there was a restaurant down the street from my house named Killer Shrimp. The franchise downsized a while ago and my local outpost closed, but the vivid memory I have of eating there, and of the piquant medley of superb flavors hitting my mouth, led by a rush of garlic and butter, is still very much alive. Can you tell? They served an oversized bowl of shrimp in an incredibly delicious and addictive spicy garlic sauce. It was the only thing on the menu, and it was served with either rice or pasta plus fresh French bread. To me, the shrimp was almost an excuse to mop up the sauce with the bread and eventually, I boiled the experience down to that most elemental and immensely satisfying taste experience. Never mind the shrimp, I just wanted to dip the bread in the sauce. Though they still have a restaurant in Marina del Rey, I rarely get to that part of town, and I needed a substitute fix. So I came up with this Spicy Killer Shrimp Soup. The broth is a divine combination of strong and satisfying flavors and a super choice for a summer night when you want to eat outdoors. Balance this with an Asian cucumber salad for that sweet and spicy combination, and you're all set.

Spicy Killer Shrimp Soup

SERVES **4**   HANDS-ON **15 MINUTES**   TOTAL **35 MINUTES**

1 Whisk together the wine and tomato paste in a medium saucepan until the tomato paste dissolves. Stir in the broth, fennel seeds, salt, cayenne pepper, paprika, bay leaf, and thyme sprig; bring to a boil over medium-high. Reduce the heat to medium-low, and simmer until slightly reduced and very flavorful, about 15 minutes.

2 Pour the broth mixture through a fine wire-mesh strainer into a clean saucepan; discard the solids. Add the coconut milk, lemon zest, and lemon juice to the broth mixture; bring to a simmer over medium. Add the shrimp, and simmer until the shrimp are just cooked through, about 3 minutes. Remove from the heat, and add the butter, stirring until the butter melts. Serve the soup in shallow bowls, and sprinkle with the parsley.

1 cup dry white wine

1 tablespoon tomato paste

1 quart chicken broth

1 tablespoon fennel seeds

1 teaspoon kosher salt

1 teaspoon cayenne pepper

½ teaspoon paprika

1 bay leaf

1 thyme sprig

1 (15-ounce) can unsweetened coconut milk

1½ teaspoons lemon zest, plus 2 tablespoons fresh lemon juice

1 pound peeled and deveined large raw shrimp, tails removed

4 tablespoons unsalted butter, cut into tablespoons

2 tablespoons chopped fresh flat-leaf parsley

◇ **VARIATION** ◇

Have a shellfish allergy? No problem. Use chunks of any type of white fish instead.

2 (2-pound) lobsters, steamed

¼ cup unsalted butter

½ cup dry sherry

¼ cup chopped celery

3 garlic cloves, smashed

2 fresh bay leaves

1 teaspoon black peppercorns

4 cups plus 2 tablespoons water

1 teaspoon kosher salt

1 cup chopped onion

½ cup chopped carrot

¼ cup chopped button mushrooms

⅛ teaspoon cayenne pepper

¾ cup whole milk

¾ cup heavy cream

½ cup dry white wine

2 tablespoons cornstarch

2 tablespoons chopped fresh chives

┌ MAKE AHEAD ┐

You can make the lobster stock up to
3 days in advance.

⟋ COOKING TIP ⟍
You can ask your local seafood market to
steam the lobster for you to save yourself
some time and hassle.

Lobster bisque is one of those items on the menu that I love but
can't bring myself to order, and yet I will instead nudge Tom to
get it and then proceed to consume at least half his portion. Over
the years, we've tasted different versions across the country, and
I sought to combine the best elements in mine, starting with the
strong suggestion of dry sherry (or very dry white wine). But that's
getting ahead of myself. I need to tell you at the outset that all the
reducing and simmering required here is worth the end result. The
lobster stock can be made several days in advance, but I prefer to
make mine the same day, all at once in fact, as it fills the kitchen with
a rich, lobstery aroma that promises something fabulous, and then
indeed delivers abundant flavor. Imagine: Cream. Butter. Lobster.
Sherry. This is rich enough to serve as a full meal along with French
bread and white wine. The rich, flavor-forward bisque will transport
you up the New England coast.

Lobster Bisque

SERVES **6**   HANDS-ON **45 MINUTES**   TOTAL **1 HOUR, 5 MINUTES**

1 Twist off the claws and tails from the lobsters. Remove the meat,
discarding the green tomalley and reserving the shells. Coarsely chop the
meat to measure about 2½ cups, and transfer to a bowl; cover and chill.

2 Melt 2 tablespoons of the butter in a Dutch oven over medium. Add the
lobster shells, and cook, stirring often, until lightly browned, about 8
minutes. Stir in the sherry, and cook until the liquid is nearly evaporated,
about 2 minutes. Add the celery, garlic, bay leaves, peppercorns, 4 cups of
the water, and ½ teaspoon of the salt. Increase the heat to high, and bring to
a boil. Reduce the heat to medium-low, and simmer until reduced to about
2½ cups, about 15 to 20 minutes. Pour through a fine wire-mesh strainer
into a bowl; discard the solids. Return the stock to the Dutch oven.

3 Meanwhile, melt the remaining 2 tablespoons butter in a medium skillet
over medium. Add the onion, carrot, mushrooms, cayenne pepper, and
the remaining ½ teaspoon salt. Cook, stirring occasionally, until the
vegetables are tender, about 10 minutes. Add the vegetable mixture to the
stock; bring to a boil over medium-high. Reduce the heat to medium-low,
and simmer until reduced to about 2 cups, about 10 minutes. Remove
from the heat.

4 Process the mixture with an immersion blender until smooth. Stir in the
milk, cream, wine, and the lobster meat; bring to a simmer over medium.
Stir together the cornstarch and the remaining 2 tablespoons water in a
small bowl; add to the soup mixture, and cook, stirring constantly, until
thickened, about 2 minutes. Garnish the servings with the chives.

One afternoon, while enjoying some reheated minestrone I'd made a couple days earlier, I grew curious about this soup's origins and learned it can be traced back to the Latins, the earliest inhabitants of Rome, when vegetables were the staples of the daily diet. I also pictured my great-grandmother, and her mother before her, making their own versions of minestrone with vegetables they either grew or got from their village markets. This soup has me continuing that tradition. It's simple, basic, and good, and watching—or rather smelling—it come together is nearly as good as the finished product. With carrots, zucchini, tomatoes, and beans simmering amid garlic cloves, crushed red pepper, onion, salt, pepper, and red wine vinegar, the more that's added, in fact, the better this gets. Thick and fortifying, this soup can be dinner on a blustery fall night. I like a dash of Sriracha for an extra kick, but I also suggest bringing this ancient victual into the 21st century with a thick grilled cheese sandwich on the side. Then, as I did, reheat the leftovers for lunch.

Vegetarian Minestrone

SERVES 4 AS A MAIN DISH, 10 AS AN APPETIZER
HANDS-ON 25 MINUTES   TOTAL 45 MINUTES

1 Heat the oil in a large Dutch oven over medium-high. Add the onion, carrot, celery, garlic, salt, rosemary, black pepper, and crushed red pepper. Cook, stirring occasionally, until the vegetables are just tender, about 8 minutes.

2 Stir in the broth, water, cannellini beans, tomatoes, zucchini, and vinegar. Bring to a boil over medium-high; reduce the heat to medium-low, and simmer until the zucchini is just tender, about 10 minutes. Stir in the collard greens, and simmer until the greens are tender, about 2 minutes. Stir in the orzo. Top with the shredded Parmesan.

2 tablespoons olive oil

1 cup chopped yellow onion

½ cup chopped carrot

¼ cup chopped celery

3 garlic cloves, chopped

2 teaspoons kosher salt

1 teaspoon chopped fresh rosemary

½ teaspoon black pepper

¼ teaspoon crushed red pepper

3 cups vegetable broth

2 cups water

1 (15.5-ounce) can cannellini beans, drained and rinsed

1 (14.5-ounce) can diced tomatoes, drained

1½ cups chopped zucchini

1 tablespoon red wine vinegar

3 cups chopped collard greens (stems removed)

2 cups cooked orzo

½ cup shredded fresh Parmesan cheese

MAKE AHEAD

This freezes well, although I'd perhaps add the collard greens during reheating.

4 cups chicken broth

2 (15-ounce) cans diced tomatoes, undrained

1 (10-ounce) can tomato sauce

1 medium white onion, diced

1 tablespoon chopped fresh garlic

1½ teaspoons kosher salt

1 teaspoon black pepper

¾ cup chopped fresh basil

5 tablespoons salted butter

¼ cup all-purpose flour

1 cup heavy cream

2 cups shredded fresh Parmesan cheese (about 8 ounces)

4 soft white bread slices

4 American cheese slices

MAKE AHEAD

You can freeze this soup for up to 3 months, so make a few batches of it.

VARIATION

Give the croutons an upgrade by using sharp Cheddar or Manchego cheese.

Some things never change. When I get a taste for soup, my thoughts immediately go back to my mom opening a can of Campbell's tomato soup and fixing a grilled cheese sandwich to go with it. How many people have had that same meal over generations? If America had a collective recipe box, this would be in it. Tens of millions of kids have been served this soup when they come in from a rainy day or hunker down next to the fireplace with a good book. I wanted to pay homage to that experience, but instead of a sandwich, I thought grilled cheese croutons would be a fun, slightly decadent twist on the tradition. This soup itself is creamy and comforting—and takes practically no time to make. Serve with a salad to keep the meal light and refreshing. You'll smile, and so will everyone at the table.

Tomato Soup with Grilled Cheese Croutons

SERVES **4 AS A MAIN DISH, 10 AS AN APPETIZER**
HANDS-ON **25 MINUTES**   TOTAL **1 HOUR**

1 Combine the broth, diced tomatoes, tomato sauce, onion, garlic, salt, pepper, and ¼ cup of the basil in a large Dutch oven over medium-low. Cook, stirring occasionally, until the onion and garlic are softened, about 30 minutes. Puree the soup with an immersion blender until smooth.

2 Melt 3 tablespoons of the butter in a medium skillet over medium. Whisk in the flour, and cook, whisking constantly, until the mixture is lightly browned, about 2 minutes. Gradually whisk in the heavy cream, whisking until the mixture is thickened and smooth. Gradually stir the cream mixture and Parmesan into the tomato mixture; cook, stirring occasionally, over medium-low until the cheese melts and is well incorporated, about 15 minutes.

3 Meanwhile, melt the remaining 2 tablespoons butter in a medium skillet until foamy. Place 2 bread slices in the skillet; top each bread slice with 2 American cheese slices, 2 tablespoons of the chopped basil, and 1 bread slice. Cook until the bread is golden brown and the cheese melts, about 3 minutes per side. Cut each sandwich into 9 pieces. Serve the soup with the croutons, and sprinkle with the remaining ¼ cup basil.

A SIDE NOTE

As an actor, I know the value of supporting players, and the same holds true when it comes to a meal. An entrée can be great on its own, but the right side dishes elevate the entire meal to a bravura experience. Where would the hamburger be without French fries? Or tomato soup without grilled cheese? And spaghetti without garlic bread is like Han Solo minus Chewie—a less than dynamic duo.

Seriously, many great chefs will reveal that their gustatory masterpieces are inspired by the availability of fresh produce as a side dish. If you visit Italy between April and May, every fine restaurant touts the arrival of white asparagus. These tender stalks become the pillars of multicourse meals—and they are sides! On a more relatable note, I remember being little and my mom asking my brothers and me what we felt like for dinner. If someone said, "Tater Tots," which happened quite frequently, she knew the entrée was going to be Sloppy Joes. The tots elevated the Sloppy Joes to a festive level they lacked on their own.

Many summer afternoons Tom and I will be walking around a farmers' market and find fresh lettuce or fat pods of juicy snap peas and we'll have an aha moment that inspires our evening meal. My hope is the sides in this chapter will provide you with a similar spark when ideas are in short supply. I have included some of my favorite foods—broccoli, asparagus, and beets—and an assortment of other dinnertime staples, some of which I have literally copied from my mom's recipe cards. They are purposely simple but tried and true when it comes to delivering maximum satisfaction.

As far as I'm concerned, side dishes are like a side note in a speech or a presentation, more of an additional thought rather than an afterthought. They should add to the meal, not overwhelm it. To that end, I've found whether I'm serving beet salad, roasted potatoes, or a simple loaf of crusty white bread, I can enhance things even more by taking extra time to find a beautiful bowl or special platter and elegant serving utensils. The little touches of a thoughtful presentation send just the right message from eye to brain to palate. Indeed, a good side should further stimulate your appetite and, as the late great Los Angeles chef Michael Roberts once noted, reflect a sense of abundance and well-being.

One final tip: Whatever you make, remind everyone of the magic words—please and thank you. There's going to be a lot of passing.

I never knew it was so easy to make my own pickles until I tried, and since then, I haven't stopped. Preparation takes practically no time and this is especially good when made the night before; the pickle is at its crunchy best after bathing overnight in the pungent pickling brine. It fills with a mélange of tangy flavors without losing any crispiness. I recommend the firm Persian cucumbers (which I also like to eat raw) instead of the traditional fatties, but those will work, too. My reason for including something this simple? A good fresh pickle is a simply delicious accompaniment with a burger or sandwich (or a Bloody Mary). And who makes homemade pickles anymore? It's classic, like a tiny clutch with a black cocktail dress. You can't go wrong.

Quick Sweet-and-Sour Pickle Spears

MAKES 1 PINT   HANDS-ON 20 MINUTES   TOTAL 8 HOURS, 45 MINUTES, INCLUDING 8 HOURS CHILLING

6 Persian cucumbers, quartered
lengthwise

1 dill sprig

1 garlic clove, smashed

½ cup apple cider vinegar

½ cup water

3 tablespoons granulated sugar

1 teaspoon yellow mustard seeds

¾ teaspoon kosher salt

1 Combine the cucumbers, dill, and garlic in a 1-pint jar. Combine the vinegar, water, sugar, mustard seeds, and salt in a small saucepan; bring to a simmer over medium, stirring until the sugar dissolves.

2 Pour the hot vinegar mixture over the cucumber mixture in the jar; cool to room temperature. Cover with the jar lid, and chill 8 hours before serving. Store the pickles in a jar in the refrigerator for up to 2 weeks.

One day I wanted something a little bit more tart for a salad I was making for dinner. At the time I was new to pickling (this was before I even tried cucumbers), but I had a taste for onions and thought of these. Two days later, I had pickled the onions. I tossed them into my salad and it tasted exactly as I had hoped. Since then, I have served these on hamburgers and hot dogs and the occasional sandwich. I like having them available. Here's an inside scoop: It's hard to get uniformly sliced onions. To do so, I use a mandoline, which is at the top of my favorite kitchen utensils. I think it satisfies the perfectionist in me. But sometimes I'm okay with cutting the onion with a knife and enjoying the imperfection of the slices. Either way, these are winners.

½ cup water

½ cup white vinegar

2 tablespoons granulated sugar

1 teaspoon kosher salt

1 medium white or yellow onion, thinly
sliced using a mandoline

⊶ VARIATIONS ⊷

Feel free to use red onions in this pickling recipe if you prefer.

Easy Pickled Onions

SERVES 4   HANDS-ON 5 MINUTES   TOTAL 25 MINUTES

Bring the water, vinegar, sugar, and salt to a simmer in a small saucepan over medium-high. Add the onion, and return the mixture to a simmer. Remove from the heat; let stand for 15 minutes. Drain.

The cheater's way to make this is to buy the pickled beets at the store. But let's remember who we are and why we are looking at this recipe. If you're like me, you love beets and you are eager to pickle them yourself. This is a fresh, tasty salad that's even better when you know you have tackled each step, starting with the beets. The flavor you create can't be purchased in a store. That's the aspect I like most about cooking—it's the personal touch. In any event, you'll see the beets pick up a nice flavor and the feta offers a contrast in texture that literally melts on your tongue. This salad, perfect with grilled chicken, almost glows on the plate with freshness and tang. And a little secret of mine? The pickling liquid makes a nice salad dressing.

Pickled Beet Salad

SERVES **4**   HANDS-ON **30 MINUTES**
TOTAL **10 HOURS, 10 MINUTES, INCLUDING 8 HOURS CHILLING**

1 Preheat the oven to 400°F. Spread the beets in a single layer in a shallow baking pan; drizzle with 1 tablespoon of the oil, and toss gently to coat. Cover the pan tightly with aluminum foil.

2 Bake until tender, about 40 minutes. Transfer the pan to a wire rack; cool, covered, for 30 minutes.

3 Using a paper towel, gently rub the beets to remove the peels. Cut each beet into 6 wedges.

4 Combine the vinegar, honey, shallot, ginger, salt, pepper, and remaining ¼ cup oil in a 1-quart jar. Cover with the lid, and shake vigorously until combined, about 30 seconds. Add the beets; cover and chill for 8 hours or overnight.

5 Remove the beets from the jar, reserving the liquid in the jar. Place 1½ cups of the lettuce on each of 4 plates. Drizzle the pickling liquid evenly over the lettuce. Top the salads evenly with the pickled beets and feta.

1 pound assorted baby beets (about 1 inch wide), trimmed

¼ cup plus 1 tablespoon extra-virgin olive oil

½ cup apple cider vinegar

2½ tablespoons honey

2 tablespoons finely chopped shallot

1 tablespoon minced crystallized ginger

½ teaspoon kosher salt

⅛ teaspoon black pepper

6 cups loosely packed baby lettuce leaves

½ cup crumbled feta cheese

INGREDIENT NOTE
If you can't find baby beets, bigger ones will do if you peel them and cut them into smaller pieces.

MAKE AHEAD
The beets may be stored in the jar for up to 4 days.

VARIATION
You can easily substitute white wine vinegar if you don't have apple cider vinegar on hand.

PICKLED BEET SALAD
PG 195

QUICK SWEET-AND-
SOUR PICKLE SPEARS
PG 194

EASY PICKLED ONIONS
PG 194

I know broccoli salad has been around forever, but I wanted to share this particular recipe as an homage to my mom. She's the person who taught me to love vegetables, and I'm always looking for new ways to enjoy them. This dish is retro, ridiculously delicious, and respectful of this sculpted member of the cabbage family. Appearance-wise, broccoli seems like it could stem from an artist's imagination of a wild garden. But it's a workhorse vegetable: always good, always dependable, always admired dating back to its origins in 6th century BC. For some reason, this leafy green favorite has not enjoyed the comeback popularity of cauliflower or Brussels sprouts, and I can't figure out why. Maybe we can help. This recipe highlights the satisfying crunch I love and the florets soak up all the good flavors, both the sweet of the cranberries and the savory of the bacon, so that I almost forget I'm eating a vegetable. It's that good.

Broccoli Salad

SERVES **4**   HANDS-ON **10 MINUTES**   TOTAL **2 HOURS, 10 MINUTES**

Whisk together the oil, white wine vinegar, honey, and mustard in a large bowl. Add the broccoli, carrot, cranberries, and onion; gently toss to coat. Cover and chill for 2 hours. Sprinkle with the walnuts and bacon just before serving.

¼ cup extra-virgin olive oil

2 tablespoons white wine vinegar

2 tablespoons honey

2 tablespoons Dijon mustard

12 ounces fresh broccoli florets, chopped (about 2 heads)

½ cup grated carrot (about 1 large carrot)

⅓ cup sweetened dried cranberries

¼ cup chopped red onion

⅓ cup chopped toasted walnuts

4 bacon slices, cooked and crumbled

1 pound fresh cremini mushrooms, halved or quartered if large

1 pound fresh asparagus, trimmed and cut into 1-inch lengths

3 tablespoons extra-virgin olive oil

1 tablespoon kosher salt

2 dried chiles de árbol, stemmed

1 teaspoon lemon zest

INGREDIENT NOTE
To make this even quicker, use pre-ground árbol, or even cayenne pepper, if that's what you have on hand.

Three components are at play here—and I emphasize the word play. Asparagus is always on my dinner menu during its season. Mushrooms are a well-established partner for the tall, thin asparagus spears. Their woodsy flavors become more pronounced and enmeshed as they're simmered together, like two dancers forgetting their physical differences and getting lost in the music as they glide across the roasting pan. Finally, the chile-lemon salt provides the special twist that brings out the utmost of these flavors, along with adding its own lemon-spicy bite. That came about one day when I was playing with salts, trying to come up with new flavors. This recipe is me having fun in the kitchen. I infuse salts with flavors I love and see where I end up. In this case, I love lemon and I love chile, and I knew this worked as soon as I put them together. It was even better with the asparagus and mushrooms. It's wonderful served alongside chicken or pork or even as a topping over egg noodles or pappardelle.

Roasted Asparagus and Mushrooms with Chile-Lemon Salt

SERVES **4**   HANDS-ON **10 MINUTES**   TOTAL **25 MINUTES**

1 Preheat the oven to 425°F. Toss together the mushrooms, asparagus, oil, and 1½ teaspoons of the salt on a rimmed baking sheet; spread in a single layer. Bake until tender and browned in spots, about 15 minutes, stirring halfway through the baking time.

2 Process the chiles in a spice grinder until coarsely ground. Transfer to a bowl, and stir in the lemon zest and the remaining 1½ teaspoons salt.

3 Transfer the mushroom mixture to a serving bowl; sprinkle with ½ teaspoon of the chile-lemon salt. Reserve the remaining chile-lemon salt for another use.

When I travel, I bring a stack of food magazines to read for inspiration. On a particular cross-country flight, I was prepping for a new season of my TV show and saw a recipe for a parsnip gratin. I thought, "Well, parsnips are root vegetables. I love root vegetables in general. What if I just do a bunch of root vegetables all together in a gratin?" A few days later, I was basking in the creamy, cheesy glory of my latest creation. You'll do the same. You can slice your root vegetables with a knife, but I recommend using my favorite kitchen utensil, the mandoline, and then taking care to spread the thin slices evenly. This dish transforms a quartet of ordinary roasted root vegetables that might not otherwise cohabit the same baking dish into old-fashioned, crowd-pleasing comfort food. Later, you can ask, "When was the last time anyone asked for more parsnips?"

Root Vegetable Gratin

SERVES **12**   HANDS-ON **20 MINUTES**   TOTAL **2 HOURS, 5 MINUTES**

1 Preheat the oven to 400°F. Lightly grease a 13- x 9-inch baking dish. Using a mandoline or sharp knife, cut the potatoes, beet, fennel bulb, and parsnips into ⅛-inch-thick slices. Toss together the vegetable slices, salt, and ¾ cup of the cream in a large bowl.

2 Spread half of the mixture evenly in the prepared baking dish. Top with 1 cup of the Parmesan. Top evenly with the remaining vegetable mixture. Pour the remaining ¾ cup cream over the vegetables, and top with the remaining ½ cup Parmesan. Cover loosely with aluminum foil. Bake for 1 hour and 10 minutes.

3 Uncover and bake until the vegetables are tender and the cheese is golden brown, 20 to 25 minutes. Transfer to a wire rack; cool for 15 minutes before serving with some black pepper ground over the top.

2 large russet potatoes (about 1½ pounds), peeled

1 large golden beet (about 1 pound), peeled

1 large fennel bulb (about 12 ounces), trimmed

2 large parsnips (about 10 ounces), peeled

2 teaspoons kosher salt

1½ cups heavy cream

1½ cups shredded Parmesan cheese (about 6 ounces)

Freshly ground black pepper

◇ VARIATION ◇

See page 213 for my version of the traditional potato gratin.

- 1 tablespoon olive oil

- 1 pound red radishes (about 20 radishes), trimmed and halved lengthwise

- 2 thyme sprigs

- 1 rosemary sprig

- 1 garlic clove, smashed

- 1 tablespoon salted butter

- ¾ teaspoon kosher salt

INGREDIENT NOTE

I recommend finding fresh radishes; keep a bit of the stem and root for a prettier dish. I don't let my radishes sit in the fridge for more than a day after bringing them home from the store.

Like acting and art in general, cooking can often highlight the more natural complexity of an ingredient by doing as little as possible. These roasted radishes are one of those sides when simplicity is intended to underscore the perfection that's possible by doing almost nothing. I say this as a fan of radishes and someone who admittedly has times when I want to do as little as possible. Is that laziness? If so, I've owned it and turned it into an attribute because I'll tell you, I once served these at a party and the first comment I heard was, "Oh my God, you can't beat cooked radishes with salt and butter." Another friend reminisced, "My mother used to have these on the farm when she was a little girl." I'm careful not to overcook the radishes to retain their unique garden-to-table freshness. When I set this on the table, in all its buttery, salty goodness, I expect—and enjoy—a little crunchiness.

Roasted Radishes

SERVES **4**   HANDS-ON **20 MINUTES**   TOTAL **20 MINUTES**

Heat the oil in a large skillet over medium-high. Add the radishes, and cook, stirring often, until the radishes begin to brown, 2 to 4 minutes. Add the thyme, rosemary, and garlic. Cover and reduce the heat to medium-low. Cook, stirring occasionally, until the radishes are tender when pierced with a fork, 6 to 8 minutes. Add the butter and salt; cook, stirring constantly, until the butter is melted, about 1 minute.

When I make roasted beets, I might as well do a podcast. As I wash and peel the beets, I go on to whomever is nearby—my husband, Tom, my son, Wolfie, or our menagerie of pets—about the relatively undervalued attributes of these root vegetables. I can't help myself. They are loaded with vitamins and minerals and contain an abundance of health benefits, and on top of all that, of course, is their robust taste. Their hard, dirt-encrusted outer skin evokes a blue-collar sturdiness, and I like that. They are easily peeled and prepared, and the subtleness of the herbs aside, a good roasted beet dappled with kosher salt can almost be a meal unto itself. Easy and not time-consuming, this recipe frequents our table throughout the summer and fall when beets are in season and plentiful. To keep it fun, I will substitute thyme or rosemary for the tarragon and serve with chicken, pork, beef, or chop leftovers tossed into a salad.

Roasted Beets with Herbs

SERVES **4**   HANDS-ON **10 MINUTES**   TOTAL **45 MINUTES**

Preheat the oven to 425°F. Toss together the beets, oil, salt, and pepper on a large rimmed baking sheet. (Do not crowd the beets.) Bake until browned around the edges and tender when pierced with a fork, about 35 minutes. Toss with the parsley and tarragon.

2 pounds baby beets, peeled and halved

1 tablespoon olive oil

1 teaspoon kosher salt

½ teaspoon black pepper

1 tablespoon chopped fresh flat-leaf parsley

1 tablespoon chopped fresh tarragon

- 2 large yellow onions (about 2 pounds), cut into ½-inch-thick slices
- ½ cup whole milk
- 6 cups vegetable oil
- 1 cup all-purpose flour
- ¾ teaspoon kosher salt
- ½ teaspoon paprika
- ½ teaspoon cayenne pepper
- 2 large eggs, lightly beaten
- ½ teaspoon table salt

⚬ VARIATION ⚬

You can use white or sweet onions, too—whichever you prefer!

I have memories of biting into a fresh onion ring when I was a little girl, sitting at a picnic table in the backyard, while my dad tended to another round of hamburgers and hot dogs on the grill. After that delicious bite I got up from the table and danced around the backyard, before returning for a second bite of onion ring—to me, that epitomizes the definition of happy food. Those are my mom's onion rings. One bite and I wanted to dance. I feel the same way about them today, and in fact I took this straight from my mom's recipe box. I made them on my show for Tom, Wolfie, and my brother Patrick, and while they didn't get up and dance, they did ask for more. These taste like classic onion rings, but the crust is lighter than a thick, traditional batter that consumes the onion. In fact, these are intentionally onion-forward. And oh-so delicious. Get ready to make your own happy memories.

Mom's Onion Rings

SERVES **6**   HANDS-ON **30 MINUTES**   TOTAL **40 MINUTES**

1 Separate the onion slices into rings, and place in an 11- x 7-inch baking dish. Pour the milk over the onion rings. Cover and chill for 15 minutes.

2 Pour the oil into a large Dutch oven; heat over high to 360°F. Stir together the flour, kosher salt, paprika, and cayenne pepper in a shallow dish. Place the eggs in a second shallow dish. Dredge the onion rings, 1 at a time, in the flour mixture; dip in the egg mixture, and dredge again in the flour mixture. Place the coated onion rings on a baking sheet. Discard the milk.

3 Fry the onion rings, in batches, until golden brown, 3 to 4 minutes, turning once. Drain on paper towels; sprinkle evenly with the table salt. Serve the onion rings immediately, or keep warm in a 200°F oven until ready to serve.

Setting aside the impossibility of competing with the perfection of the frozen Ore-Ida originals (hey, I'm just being real), my initial fear of homemade Tater Tots was that they'd be dry and therefore disappointing. But after making these several times I am happy to report they taste exactly as I'd hoped. And beyond their starchy addictiveness, they made me feel like a kid again. Are they what my Food Network colleague Guy Fieri once called "the bomb tot?" They're close. My goal was to make a less fattening version of the fried tot, so in terms of that, check. I also wanted to experiment with a denser version where I could play with the seasoning and even combine ingredients, like grating cauliflower in with the potato to save even more calories, and so again, check. Serve with burgers, hot dogs, Sloppy Joes, or a grilled cheese sandwich—and try with a spicy ketchup. As with all tots, they're just fun to eat.

Homemade Baked Potato Tots

SERVES **12**   HANDS-ON **40 MINUTES**   TOTAL **1 HOUR, 40 MINUTES**

1 Combine the potatoes and 2 tablespoons of the salt in a large saucepan. Add water to cover the potatoes, and bring to a boil over high. Reduce the heat to medium, and cook until the potatoes are tender when pierced with a fork, 15 to 20 minutes. Drain and cool completely, 20 to 30 minutes.

2 Preheat the oven to 425°F. Lightly grease and line a baking sheet with aluminum foil. Finely shred the potatoes with a box grater. Stir together the potatoes and the egg in a medium bowl. Add the flour, and stir to combine. Stir in the cayenne pepper, smoked paprika, garlic powder, and remaining 2 teaspoons salt. Form the potato mixture into about 84 (1¼-inch-long) cylinders, and place on the prepared baking sheet. Bake until golden brown, 20 to 25 minutes.

4 russet potatoes (about 3 pounds), peeled and halved lengthwise

2 tablespoons plus 2 teaspoons kosher salt

1 large egg, lightly beaten

½ cup all-purpose flour

¾ teaspoon cayenne pepper

1 teaspoon smoked paprika

1 teaspoon garlic powder

◆ TRICK TECHNIQUE ◆

Using a box grater is easier for larger potatoes than smaller ones.

MOM'S ONION RINGS
PG 206

MICROWAVE POTATO CHIPS
PG 210

HOMEMADE BAKED
POTATO TOTS
PG 207

3 medium Yukon Gold potatoes (about 1 pound), thinly sliced using a mandoline

3 tablespoons olive oil

1 teaspoon kosher salt

〜 COOKING TIP 〜

Microwaves are different—some are more powerful than others. Depending on yours, you may need less than 4 minutes or more. So keep an eye on the first batch.

I happen to be married to a man who loves potato chips. But he has a problem. He can't just have a bag of potato chips in the house, eat a few, and put the rest in the pantry. He has to eat the entire bag. In one sitting. Making homemade potato chips is a way to address that issue. I just don't make that many. Or I make extra. It depends. The point is these are fun and delicious—well, make that delicious and irresistible—and a healthier version than the typical store-bought fried chip. The trick is to rinse the potatoes thoroughly and then get the individual slices very dry afterward. The patience required is a little painful, but so worth it. I vary these by adding rosemary or garlic or black pepper, salt and vinegar . . . whatever flavor we feel like at that moment. These are a tad time-consuming, but it's fun to say you've made your own potato chips in the microwave.

Microwave Potato Chips

SERVES **4**   HANDS-ON **20 MINUTES**   TOTAL **35 MINUTES**

1 Place the potato slices in a large bowl with cold water to cover; stir to release the starches. Drain and refill the bowl with cold water. Stir to release the starches. Repeat the process as many times as necessary until the water is clear when stirred. Line a baking sheet with paper towels. Spread the potatoes in a single layer on the prepared baking sheet. Pat dry with paper towels.

2 Line a large microwave-safe plate (the biggest one that will fit in your microwave) with 2 layers of paper towels. Arrange the potato slices in a single layer, ensuring the potatoes do not touch each other. Brush both sides of the potato slices evenly with the oil; sprinkle with the salt. Microwave on HIGH for 4 minutes. Turn the slices, and microwave on MEDIUM for 4 minutes. Microwave on LOW until crispy and golden brown in spots, about 5 minutes. Transfer the chips to a serving bowl. Repeat the process with the remaining potatoes, oil, and salt.

Here's another example of my embracing simplicity. This recipe's preparation is quick, easy, and minimal, yet it's the nuances in each of the three steps that ensure the full flavor of these red beauties is brought out to buttery perfection. Let me explain: As they're boiled, make sure the potatoes are cooked to an easy tenderness. Then, once transferred to the saucepan, instead of a gentle sail through the butter, let them crisp to a golden brown. The contrast between the roasted exterior and the soft inside provides the satisfaction in the bite. But the clincher is the dusting they receive at the end, soaking up a generous coating of salt, pepper, butter, parsley, and chives. I serve them alongside roasted chicken or steak and beans or asparagus. Get them right and people who've never paid attention to a roasted potato will perk right up.

Rissole Potatoes

SERVES **4**   HANDS-ON **20 MINUTES**   TOTAL **30 MINUTES**

1 Combine the potatoes and 2 tablespoons of the salt in a large saucepan. Add water to cover the potatoes, and bring to a boil over high. Reduce the heat to medium, and cook until the potatoes are tender when pierced with a fork, 10 to 15 minutes. Drain in a colander.

2 Melt 4 tablespoons of the butter in a saucepan over medium-high. Add the potatoes; cook, stirring occasionally, until golden brown on all sides, 10 to 12 minutes.

3 Combine the potatoes, parsley, chives, pepper, and the remaining 2 tablespoons butter and ¾ teaspoon salt in a medium bowl; toss to coat.

1½ pounds small (about 1½-inch) red potatoes

2 tablespoons plus ¾ teaspoon kosher salt

¼ cup plus 2 tablespoons salted butter, softened

2 tablespoons chopped fresh flat-leaf parsley

2 tablespoons thinly sliced fresh chives

½ teaspoon black pepper

◇ VARIATION ◇

Mix up the herbs a bit—basil, thyme, and chopped rosemary would be really nice.

When you get a craving for a rich, creamy, indulgent potato, say for a holiday family get-together or, in my case, a birthday or a book club gathering, this should be your first choice: scalloped potatoes. To slice the peeled potatoes, use a sharp knife if that's your preference, or, if you're like me, get out your mandoline and enjoy turning out perfectly round and thin cuts that can be laid flat and piled high in the baking dish. I get a kick watching this dish come together; each step is clearly defined, different, and yet essential. Now, I'm aware that a traditional scalloped potato does not include cheese, and that adding cheese to this recipe technically makes it a potato au gratin, but so what? I got this recipe from my mom, who called it Scalloped Potatoes, and out of respect for her, I'm going to continue this rich tradition of misinformation. When all is said and eaten, I think the only question you'll be asked is the same one I get afterward: "When will you make this again?"

Scalloped Potatoes

SERVES **12**   HANDS-ON **20 MINUTES**   TOTAL **2 HOURS, 15 MINUTES**

1 Preheat the oven to 375°F. Lightly grease a 13- x 9-inch baking dish. Using a mandoline or sharp knife, cut the potatoes into ⅛-inch-thick slices. Toss together the potatoes, salt, and ¾ cup of the cream in a large bowl.

2 Spread half of the potato mixture evenly in the prepared baking dish. Top evenly with 1 cup of the cheese, and shingle the remaining potato slices over the cheese. Pour the remaining ¾ cup cream evenly over the potatoes and sprinkle with the remaining ½ cup cheese. Cover loosely with aluminum foil. Bake for 1 hour and 20 minutes.

3 Uncover and bake until the potatoes are tender and the cheese is golden brown, 20 to 30 minutes. Transfer to a wire rack, and cool for 15 minutes before serving.

4 large russet potatoes (about 3¾ pounds), peeled

1½ teaspoons table salt

1½ cups heavy cream

1½ cups shredded Gruyère cheese

◇ VARIATION ◇

Don't have heavy cream on hand? Use half-and-half or even whole milk. Try Manchego instead of Gruyère cheese.

MAKE AHEAD

To get ahead, peel and cut the potatoes ahead of time but keep them in cold water so that they don't brown.

2 cups lukewarm water (about 105°F)

3 tablespoons granulated sugar

1 (¼-ounce) envelope active dry yeast

2 teaspoons kosher salt

6 cups all-purpose flour, plus more for work surface

5 tablespoons salted butter, melted

1 teaspoon olive oil

EQUIPMENT

You will need two loaf pans for this recipe or, if you have only one, roll the second half of dough into 12 equal balls and bake on a greased baking sheet for 20 minutes for dinner rolls like my grandmother did.

Restaurants do it, so why not put a basket of fresh bread on the table with dinner? Not with every meal, of course, but on those occasions when the craving strikes, this elicits an immensely satisfying response: fresh white bread warm from the oven. It's a throwback, and that's the point. With a spread of rich, salted butter melting into the soft bread, it's like treating your soul to a hug. In other words, this is pure comfort food. This simple recipe is similar to my grandmother's bread recipe except she made them into little rolls and I prefer to make it as a loaf. It's almost mistake-proof, and its crunchy crust and pillowy interior will be a hit whether you serve it plain for dinner, as French toast for breakfast, or sliced for sandwiches at lunchtime. On the slight chance you end up with days-old leftovers, make bread pudding. This is happy food.

White Bread

SERVES **18**   HANDS-ON **40 MINUTES**   TOTAL **2 HOURS, 50 MINUTES**

1 Stir together the water, sugar, and yeast in a large bowl. Let stand until foamy, about 5 minutes.

2 Stir together the salt and 3 cups of the flour. Gradually add to the yeast mixture, stirring just until combined. Stir in the melted butter.

3 Add the remaining 3 cups flour, and stir just until combined. Turn the dough out onto a lightly floured surface; knead until the dough is slightly tacky and elastic, about 10 minutes.

4 Brush the dough with the oil; place in a large bowl, cover with a clean towel, and place in a warm place (80° to 85°F), free from drafts, until the dough doubles in size, about 45 minutes.

5 Turn the dough out onto a lightly floured work surface; punch the dough down. Divide the dough in half; shape each half into an 11- x 7-inch rectangle. Place on a lightly greased baking sheet; cover and let rise for 25 minutes.

6 Preheat the oven to 375°F. Knead 1 dough half lightly, and roll into a tight log, about 12 inches long. Pinch together the ends, and tuck under the log to form a smooth top. Fit the dough log into a lightly greased 9- x 5-inch loaf pan. Repeat with the second dough half.

7 Bake until the bread reaches an internal temperature of 190°F or when the bread sounds hollow when tapped, about 40 minutes.

I like spicy food. I love mac and cheese. If you're like me, nothing more needs to be said because you already understand the basics: This is plain, old-fashioned comfort food with a little zing. It can be an entire meal rather than a side, but there are times when I'm serving roasted chicken, ham, or pork chops, and a side of mac and cheese, with some green beans or spinach, is an ideal accompaniment. I also have quite a few good friends from the South who will argue that there are actually six basic food groups: meat, dairy, grains, fruits, vegetables, and mac and cheese. There have been more than a few meals in my life when I'd support that claim, including the first time I added the spicy twist to this recipe. This is super simple and not a boxed recipe—it's homemade and you can use any flavor potato chip on the top. Serve this as a side or enjoy it by itself with a salad. Either way, I promise no one will complain.

Spicy Mac 'n' Cheese

SERVES **8**   HANDS-ON **30 MINUTES**   TOTAL **45 MINUTES**

1 Preheat the oven to 425°F. Cook the pasta according to the package directions; drain.

2 While the pasta cooks, melt the butter in a stockpot over medium-high. Add the onion and jalapeños, and cook, stirring occasionally, until tender, 5 to 6 minutes. Add the flour, and cook, stirring constantly, for 1 minute. Stir in the milk and bring to a boil. Reduce the heat to medium; cook, stirring occasionally, until slightly thickened, 2 to 3 minutes. Remove from the heat.

3 Add the onion dip, hot sauce, salt, pepper, and 12 ounces of the cheese to the onion mixture; stir until the cheese is melted. Add the hot cooked pasta; stir to coat. Stir in the remaining 4 ounces cheese. Spread the mixture evenly in a 13- x 9-inch baking dish coated with cooking spray. Sprinkle evenly with the crushed chips. Bake until the top is lightly browned, about 15 minutes. Sprinkle with extra jalapeño, and serve immediately.

1 pound uncooked pasta (such as penne, cavatappi, or rotini)

6 tablespoons salted butter

1 small yellow onion, chopped

2 jalapeño chiles, chopped, plus more for garnish

5 tablespoons all-purpose flour

1 quart whole milk

2 tablespoons creamy French onion dip

1 tablespoon hot sauce

1½ teaspoons kosher salt

½ teaspoon black pepper

2 (8-ounce) packages shredded extra-sharp Cheddar cheese

2 cups crushed salt and vinegar potato chips

⊳ VARIATION ⊲

Change up the toppings: plain or jalapeño potato chips or a mix of all.

1 (¾-pound) smoked ham shank

1 pound dried red beans

½ pound andouille sausage, chopped

3 celery stalks, chopped

1 medium yellow onion, chopped

1 large green bell pepper, chopped

1 tablespoon chili powder

2 teaspoons kosher salt

1 teaspoon ground cumin

1 teaspoon garlic powder

½ to 1 teaspoon cayenne pepper, depending on your spice level

½ teaspoon onion powder

½ teaspoon paprika

½ teaspoon light brown sugar

4 cups chicken stock

8 cups cooked long-grain white rice

4 scallions, chopped

I have two wonderful Louisiana girls in my life, my sister-in-law Stacy and my dear friend Faith Ford, and both are extraordinarily good cooks who make red beans and rice that has a similar effect on me. Seconds after the spoon goes in my mouth and the red beans and rice settle on my tongue, I have an almost involuntary reaction. My eyes shut, my brain tells my entire body that something incredible is happening, and I moan, "Oh my God, this is good." The truth is, this is another one of those easy slow-cooker recipes—more assembly than cooking—that not only saves time but uses that time ever so generously in enabling the ham and the andouille sausage and the spices and the beans and the rice to all mingle and absorb the different flavors, producing that OMG effect. This is like gumbo, but easier. Typically, I will serve this to Tom and myself on Sundays as we watch football. Quite often, we will enjoy this as a meal in itself.

Slow-Cooker Red Beans and Rice

SERVES **8 TO 10**   HANDS-ON **15 MINUTES**
TOTAL **5 HOURS, 15 MINUTES**

1   Combine the ham shank, red beans, andouille, celery, onion, bell pepper, chili powder, salt, cumin, garlic powder, cayenne, onion powder, paprika, and brown sugar in a 6-quart slow cooker. Add the chicken stock, and stir to combine. Cover and cook on HIGH until the beans are tender, 5 to 7 hours.

2   Remove the ham shank; shred the meat, and return the meat to the slow cooker. Discard the bone. Serve the red bean mixture with the rice, and top the servings with the scallions.

CHAPTER 6

FINISHING SWEET

Ah, dessert. When I was a child, my parents told me to save room for dessert, and now I often anticipate this part of the meal before my first forkful of salad. Once the taste for ice cream or pie sets in, it's difficult to think of anything else. But dessert is tricky. If it's not sweet enough, all that came before is likely to be overshadowed by a disappointing ending. If it's overwrought, there's a risk of sending people into a sugar coma.

My take on planning dessert is similar to a story a producer once told about hiring screenwriters. He said there are 5,000 people in Hollywood who are able to write the opening of a great screenplay. But there are only a handful that know how to finish them in a way that delivers at the box office. The same is true when it comes to dessert. Nearly everyone can get the first couple courses right. But it's hard to finish sweet.

Many fine restaurants offer desserts that are too complicated for my taste. Looking through the menu can be intimidating. Favorites get deconstructed, a dollop of whipped cream set in a spoon, the icing smeared on the side of a plate, berries set next to a sliver of crust—that sort of thing. When all I want is a slice of cake, a bowl of ice cream, or a homemade brownie like my mom used to serve at the end of a meal.

There are, of course, chefs who get it right by keeping it simple. Bread pudding. Banana cream pie. Hot fudge sundaes. Cake. Blondies. These work for me even in the fanciest establishments. So I don't sound overly critical, I want to state that some remarkable things have happened recently in the world of desserts. Like the pairing of salt and caramel. At the end of a meal, all a waiter has to do is mention "salted caramel" anything and I'm in. What took 2,017 years for human beings to figure out that this combo is impossibly delicious?

However, for as much as I think about dessert, I'm not a genuine dessert person. I know quite a few people who are; they can't walk past a tray of sweets without taking one or two and stressing about whether to have a third. I understand. But when I was growing up my mom made desserts only on special occasions, like birthdays and holidays, and cookies when inspiration struck or at Christmastime. Sweets weren't her thing.

Likewise, I can take dessert or leave it. But when I take it, I have a simple rule. It has to be worth it. It better be really, really good. I want to enjoy every bite. I want dinner, like a great movie, to come to a satisfying and sweet conclusion. The desserts I've included here meet that standard. They are true favorites of mine: cakes, cookies, a granita, ice cream sandwiches, a cannoli (how could I not include?), and even popcorn. As you're no doubt aware, I'm a sucker for lemon anything, so I've also chosen a few desserts that offer a lemon-flavored lift. None of these are the fanciest, but they meet my criteria.

They are really, really good—and worth it.

All I can do here is issue a warning: Get ready for an amazing, tasty, and addictive treat—and only eat these if you're with someone who won't mind your licking your fingers. I was actually trying to come up with a peanut butter and jelly popcorn, an idea I have not yet been able to perfect, but that doesn't mean I won't try again one day. . . Anyway, I got so frustrated in my show's crash kitchen for an episode that was supposed to be about dining outside that I finally tossed my experiment out and someone said, "Well, how about s'mores? Let's try to make that into popcorn." A few minutes later, I had tossed all the ingredients in a large bowl and then poured the hot sugar mixture over the popcorn, marshmallows, and chocolate chips. As it cooled, I couldn't hold back any longer. I had to taste, and when I did, the sweet and salty combo on the popcorn blew my mind. It's much better if you let it cool for an hour. Also, mix it well—don't let all the chocolate settle on the bottom. And yes, this does save in an airtight container, but good luck with that.

S'mores Popcorn

SERVES **16**   HANDS-ON **25 MINUTES**   TOTAL **1 HOUR, 45 MINUTES**

1 Preheat the oven to 250°F. Line 2 large rimmed baking sheets with parchment paper or silicone baking mats.

2 Toss together the popcorn, marshmallows, graham crackers, and chocolate chips in a large bowl.

3 Combine the granulated sugar, butter, brown sugar, and corn syrup in a medium saucepan. Bring to a boil over medium-high, stirring until the butter melts and the ingredients are completely combined. Continue to boil, without stirring, until a candy thermometer inserted in the mixture registers 245°F (firm ball stage), about 4 minutes. Remove the sugar mixture from the heat, and stir in the salt and baking soda. Gradually pour the sugar mixture over the popcorn mixture, stirring gently with a heatproof spatula until the popcorn is evenly coated. Spread evenly onto the prepared baking sheets.

4 Bake until the sugar mixture is melted and evenly incorporated, about 20 minutes, stirring gently after 10 minutes. Remove from the oven, and place in a cool, dry place until the chocolate is firm, about 1 hour.

10 cups popped salted popcorn

1 cup miniature marshmallows

1 cup lightly crushed graham crackers (about 5 rectangles)

¾ cup semisweet chocolate chips

¾ cup granulated sugar

½ cup unsalted butter

¼ cup packed light brown sugar

¼ cup light corn syrup

1 teaspoon kosher salt

½ teaspoon baking soda

EQUIPMENT

You will need a candy thermometer for this recipe.

3½ cups water

1 cup granulated sugar

2 (1-ounce) packages basil leaves and stems

⅓ cup fresh lemon juice (from 2 lemons)

¼ cup vodka (optional)

Small fresh basil leaves

MAKE AHEAD

Once you move past the scraping stage, this granita will keep in the freezer for up to a week.

Delicious and super easy—that's all you need to know, and it hits the spot at the end of a pool party or cookout. With me, lemon and basil go hand in hand, and there's nothing better than a dessert that actually leaves you feeling light and refreshed. To change this up, use lime juice instead of lemon and make frozen basil limeade granita. As for the basil, steep the entire package in the simple syrup; quite a bit of flavor comes from the stems and this is all about putting the flavor of the lemon and basil front and center. One other idea: Pour a little vodka over it and you have a delicious summer cocktail.

Lemon-Basil Granita

SERVES **6**   HANDS-ON **15 MINUTES**
TOTAL **6 HOURS, INCLUDING 5 HOURS FREEZING**

1 Combine the water, sugar, and basil in a medium saucepan; bring to a boil over medium-high, stirring until the sugar dissolves completely. Remove from the heat, and cool to room temperature, about 30 minutes.

2 Pour the mixture through a fine wire-mesh strainer into a 13- x 9-inch baking dish; discard the basil leaves and stems. Stir in the lemon juice and, if desired, the vodka. Freeze until just beginning to harden, about 2 hours.

3 Scrape with a fork to form small crystals, and freeze until fully frozen, about 3 hours, scraping with a fork at 1-hour intervals. Serve the granita in chilled glasses, and garnish with the small basil leaves.

If you're picturing someone standing in her pajamas before watching a movie, dipping a pretzel in a jar of peanut butter and a can of chocolate sauce and then having a eureka moment, I will neither confirm nor deny the origin of this dessert. I will say that it's slightly more involved than that description, or perhaps I should say it's more evolved. Melt chocolate chips, dip ordinary pretzels of your choosing, and then pipe the peanut butter mixture and voilà, you have a nighttime treat that tastes like Reese's Pieces. For variety, try butterscotch chips, white chocolate chips, or different types of chocolate. All of them have the same smile-inducing effect. They're easy and dangerously good.

Peanut Butter Chocolate Pretzels

SERVES **8**   HANDS-ON **30 MINUTES**   TOTAL **1 HOUR, 15 MINUTES**

1 Place the chocolate chips and 1 tablespoon of the shortening in a small microwave-safe bowl; microwave on HIGH until melted and smooth, about 1 to 1½ minutes, stirring every 30 seconds.

2 Using a fork, dip the pretzels, 1 at a time, into the melted chocolate; let the excess chocolate drip off. Place on a baking sheet lined with parchment paper. Chill until the chocolate is set, about 30 minutes.

3 Place the peanut butter chips and remaining ½ tablespoon shortening in a small microwave-safe bowl; microwave on HIGH until melted and smooth, about 45 seconds to 1 minute, stirring after 30 seconds. Spoon the mixture into a ziplock plastic bag; snip 1 corner of the bag, and squeeze to drizzle the peanut butter mixture over the pretzels. Chill until the peanut butter drizzle is set, about 15 minutes.

1 cup semisweet chocolate chips

1½ tablespoons vegetable shortening

3 cups miniature pretzel twists (about 4 ounces)

½ cup peanut butter chips

MAKE AHEAD

These can be made ahead and stored in an airtight container in a cool place for up to a week.

3 cups all-purpose flour

1 teaspoon baking powder

½ teaspoon baking soda

¼ teaspoon table salt

1 cup unsalted butter, softened

1 cup packed light brown sugar

½ cup granulated sugar

2 large eggs

1½ teaspoons vanilla extract

1 cup caramel bits

¾ cup semisweet chocolate chips

1½ teaspoons flaked sea salt

MAKE AHEAD

These can be made ahead and stored in an airtight container in a cool place for up to a week.

The Astaire and Rogers of dessert ingredients, salted caramel makes chocolate taste even better and chocolate helps salted caramel soar beyond its potential as a solo act. To me, the marriage of these two in a cookie was inevitable. It happened when I was at a farmers' market one Sunday and saw a booth with homemade candy, including perhaps the best caramel I'd ever tasted. A light went off. "I'm going to get the best caramel," I told myself, "slice it up into little chunks, and put it in chocolate chip cookies. It's going to be amazing." And it was—except the caramel chunks melted and burned around the edges. After several variations, I settled on using the Kraft caramel bits from the baking aisle in the grocery store. They held their shape and the taste was everything I found in the original try. Enjoy.

Salted Caramel Chocolate Chip Cookies

MAKES **3 DOZEN**   HANDS-ON **10 MINUTES**   TOTAL **1 HOUR, 15 MINUTES**

1 Preheat the oven to 375°F. Position the racks in the upper third and lower third of the oven. Line 2 large baking sheets with parchment paper. Whisk together the flour, baking powder, baking soda, and salt in a bowl.

2 Combine the butter, brown sugar, and granulated sugar in a large bowl; beat with an electric mixer at medium speed until light and fluffy, about 3 minutes. Add the eggs, 1 at a time, beating well after each addition. Add the vanilla, and beat until combined. Add the flour mixture, and beat until just incorporated. Stir in the caramel bits and chocolate chips.

3 Drop the dough by heaping tablespoonfuls 2 inches apart onto the prepared baking sheets. Sprinkle each cookie with a pinch of sea salt.

4 Bake until golden brown, about 13 minutes, switching the baking sheets top rack to bottom rack halfway through. Cool the cookies on the baking sheets for 3 to 5 minutes. Transfer the cookies to a wire rack to cool completely. Repeat the procedure with remaining cookie dough.

My mother-in-law, Helen, first introduced me to these cookies. I tinkered slightly but the credit belongs to her. She always had cookies in her suburban Ohio home when I visited before Tom and I were married, and this ricotta cookie with sour cream glaze was my favorite. I say they were hot in Cleveland. They're tender and buttery, and melt in your mouth. I like one or two with a cup of coffee in the afternoon; after dinner, an espresso only heightens the simple goodness.

Ricotta Cookies with Sour Cream Glaze

MAKES **ABOUT 2½ DOZEN**   HANDS-ON **25 MINUTES**   TOTAL **1 HOUR**

1 Make the Ricotta Cookies: Preheat the oven to 350°F. Whisk together the flour, baking soda, and salt in a small bowl. Beat the butter and sugar with an electric mixer at medium speed until light and fluffy, 2 to 3 minutes. Beat in the ricotta, lemon zest, and vanilla. Add the eggs, 1 at a time, beating until blended after each addition. Gradually add the flour mixture, beating at low speed until blended. Drop the dough by tablespoonfuls 2 inches apart onto large baking sheets lined with parchment paper.

2 Bake until the cookies are set and golden around the edges, rotating the pans as needed, about 12 minutes. Cool the cookies on the pans 5 minutes; remove from the pans to wire racks, and cool completely, about 20 minutes.

3 Make the Sour Cream Glaze: Whisk together the powdered sugar, sour cream, butter, and vanilla until smooth. Spread evenly over the cooled cookies; sprinkle with the toasted almonds.

RICOTTA COOKIES

2 cups all-purpose flour

½ teaspoon baking soda

½ teaspoon kosher salt

1 cup unsalted butter, softened

1 cup granulated sugar

8 ounces ricotta cheese (about 1 cup)

1 teaspoon lemon zest (from 1 lemon)

1 teaspoon vanilla extract

2 large eggs

SOUR CREAM GLAZE

1½ cups powdered sugar

¼ cup sour cream

2 tablespoons unsalted butter, melted

½ teaspoon vanilla extract

½ cup sliced almonds, toasted

SALTED CARAMEL
CHOCOLATE CHIP COOKIES
PG 232

MOM'S CHRISTMAS BELLS
PG 236

RICOTTA COOKIES WITH
SOUR CREAM GLAZE
PG 233

Every year my mom made Christmas cookies, in a variety of types, shapes, and sizes, and every year I pined for these Christmas bells. Ironically these were her least favorite to make—but only because they required more time than the others. There are a few extra steps here, but I can still hear myself saying, "Please, please, please, they're so good." My favorite part was and remains filling the cone-shaped cookie with the buttery pecan stuffing, baking for a few more minutes, and then anticipating that first delicious bite as they cool. I've added a few spices and orange zest to the cookie that weren't in my mom's original recipe, giving these more flavor. They're perfect for a Christmas cookie swap or just to have as treats in the house during the holidays.

Mom's Christmas Bells

MAKES **4½ DOZEN**   HANDS-ON **25 MINUTES**
TOTAL **3 HOURS, INCLUDING 2 HOURS CHILLING**

1 Make the Dough: Preheat the oven to 350°F. Beat the brown sugar and butter with an electric mixer at medium speed until light and fluffy, about 3 minutes. Beat in the corn syrup, egg, cream, and lemon zest. Whisk together the flour, instant espresso, ginger, cinnamon, baking soda, and salt in a separate bowl; gradually add to the butter mixture, and beat at low speed until combined. Shape the dough into a flat disk; wrap with the plastic wrap. Chill the dough until firm, at least 2 hours.

2 Make the Filling: Stir together the brown sugar, maraschino cherry juice, and butter until blended; stir in the pecans.

3 Roll the dough to ⅛-inch thickness on a lightly floured surface. Cut with a 2½-inch round cookie cutter. Place the dough circles 2 inches apart on ungreased baking sheets.

4 Place ½ teaspoon of the filling in the center of each dough circle. Shape into a cone by folding the edges of the dough to meet over the filling; pinch the edges together. Place 1 cherry half at the opening end of each bell for the clapper.

5 Bake until golden brown, about 12 minutes. Cool on the pans for 5 minutes; remove to a wire rack to cool completely.

DOUGH

1¼ cups packed dark brown sugar

1 cup unsalted butter, softened

¼ cup dark corn syrup

1 large egg

1 tablespoon heavy cream

1½ teaspoons lemon zest (from 1 large lemon)

3¼ cups all-purpose flour, plus more for work surface

1 tablespoon instant espresso

1½ teaspoons ground ginger

1 teaspoon ground cinnamon

½ teaspoon baking soda

½ teaspoon table salt

FILLING

⅓ cup packed dark brown sugar

1 tablespoon maraschino cherry juice (from jar)

1 tablespoon unsalted butter, softened

1½ cups finely chopped toasted pecans

27 maraschino cherries without stems, halved (from 2 [10-ounce] jars)

What you're going to need is a napkin—or two. The best way to eat these chocolate peppermint ice-cream sandwiches is with your hands, after letting them sit out a few minutes to get the ice cream a little soft. It puts all the flavor in each bite. But I'm getting ahead of myself. One day I made a chocolate peppermint cookie; they're wafer thin and a pain to make, but the intense chocolate-peppermint flavor that's packed in this cookie is ridiculously good and so worth the effort. Indeed, as I stared at these cooling on the kitchen counter, I thought, "These would taste even better with some ice cream." I was right and they ended up as a sandwich because the cookies could be made a little bit thicker, which made the dough easier to work with and only increased the flavor.

Chocolate Peppermint Ice-Cream Sandwiches

SERVES **16**   HANDS-ON **30 MINUTES**   TOTAL **3 HOURS, 5 MINUTES**

1 Preheat the oven to 350°F. Position the racks in the upper third and lower third of the oven. Line 2 large baking sheets with parchment paper.

2 Whisk together the flour, cocoa, baking soda, and salt in a medium bowl; set aside.

3 Beat the sugar and butter with an electric mixer at medium-high speed until light and fluffy, about 3 minutes. Add the egg, vanilla, and peppermint extract, and beat until just combined. Beat in the flour mixture at low speed until the dough comes together. Divide the dough in half, and press each half into a flat disk (about 1 inch thick). Wrap with the plastic wrap, and chill until almost firm, about 1 hour.

4 Roll 1 dough disk to ¼-inch thickness on a lightly floured surface. Cut the dough into 10 rounds using a 2½-inch round or fluted cutter; place the dough rounds ½ inch apart on the prepared baking sheet. Refrigerate the dough scraps. Repeat the procedure with remaining dough disk.

5 Bake the dough rounds until slightly puffed, about 10 minutes, switching top rack to bottom rack after 5 minutes. Cool on the baking sheets for 5 minutes. Transfer the cookies to a wire rack, and cool completely, about 20 minutes. (The cookies will crisp as they cool.) Keep the oven on.

6 Meanwhile, gather the dough scraps together, and roll to ¼-inch thickness on a lightly floured surface. Cut 12 additional rounds using the cutter; discard any remaining scraps, and repeat the baking and cooling process.

7 Place about ¼ cup of the ice cream onto the bottoms of half of the cookies; top with remaining cookies, and roll the edges in sprinkles. Place on a baking sheet lined with parchment paper, and freeze until firm, about 1 hour. To keep, wrap these individually and freeze for up to 2 weeks.

2¼ cups all-purpose flour, plus more for work surface

½ cup unsweetened cocoa

½ teaspoon baking soda

½ teaspoon kosher salt

1¼ cups granulated sugar

1 cup unsalted butter, softened

1 large egg

1 teaspoon vanilla extract

1 teaspoon peppermint extract

4 cups peppermint ice cream or vanilla ice cream, slightly softened

¼ cup pink candy sprinkles or nonpareils

⌐ VARIATION ⌐

For a change, omit the peppermint from the chocolate cookie and use your favorite flavor of ice cream. Even roll in chopped nuts instead of sprinkles. Your call.

ZEPPOLE

Vegetable oil

1 cup all-purpose flour

2 tablespoons granulated sugar

1 teaspoon baking soda

½ teaspoon kosher salt

¼ teaspoon ground cinnamon

1 cup ricotta cheese

2 large eggs, lightly beaten

1 teaspoon orange zest

½ teaspoon vanilla extract

Powdered sugar

MARSALA SAUCE

1 cup packed light brown sugar

½ cup unsalted butter

¼ cup sweet Marsala

⌐ VARIATION ¬

I have also tossed the zeppole in cinnamon-sugar, but prefer powdered sugar.

⌐ COOKING TIP ⌐

Use a fry thermometer as it's important to keep the oil at 350°F—too high and they will burn on the outside and the inside will be raw; too low and the zeppole will be too oily.

I first had zeppole at one of Mario Batali's restaurants, and I fell in love. What wasn't to love? They were light, sweet, miniature balls of dough lightly fried until the outer skin was ever so gently crisped, sweetened, and drizzled with a yummy berry compote. And what I thought when my brain wasn't dizzy with pleasure was, "Oh, I can have donuts after dinner if they're called zeppole instead?" Yes, zeppole are tiny fried Italian pastries that remind me of donut holes, and for some reason, eating them after dinner doesn't feel as decadent as eating donuts for breakfast. The zeppole I make taste like a moist funnel cake, the ricotta and orange zest being particular favorite flavors of mine here, and the sauce is similar to a sweet marsala. (It could also be a great topping for ice cream, cake, or bread pudding.) Don't let the fact that these require frying in a pan of hot oil and separate steps for the sauce intimidate you. It all goes quickly and easily and ends up an impressive and tasty way to finish off a meal, what I'll describe as the dessert equivalent of a heartfelt goodbye kiss on the cheek.

Mini Zeppole with Marsala Sauce

SERVES **6**   HANDS-ON **30 MINUTES**   TOTAL **30 MINUTES**

1 First make the Zeppole: Pour the oil to a depth of 2 inches into a large, wide pot. Heat over medium-high to 350°F.

2 Meanwhile, whisk together the flour, sugar, baking soda, salt, and cinnamon in a large bowl. Add the ricotta, eggs, orange zest, and vanilla; stir until just combined.

3 Working in batches, carefully drop the batter by tablespoonfuls into the hot oil, and fry until puffed and golden brown, 1 to 2 minutes per batch. Transfer to a paper towel-lined rimmed baking sheet; drain. Repeat the procedure with remaining batter, returning the oil to 350°F between batches.

4 Meanwhile, make the Marsala Sauce: Bring all the ingredients to a boil in a medium saucepan over medium-high, stirring often. Cook until the sugar dissolves and the sauce is smooth, 1 to 2 minutes.

5 Dust the zeppole generously with the powdered sugar, and serve immediately with the Marsala Sauce on the side.

I have the impression that many people are scared of making cannoli at home, but there's no reason. These should be part of your special occasion dessert repertoire, no different than cakes or brownies. There are basically two steps—making the shells and filling them. But never fill a cannoli shell until it's ready to be served. Any bakery worth its sugar will finish their cannoli only when you order them. Otherwise the shells get soggy. I am fairly traditional when it comes to making the shells; like my mom and grandmother, I roll out the dough, cut a circle, and create the shell using a cannoli tube. But occasionally I'll use my pizzelle maker—the device normally used for traditional Italian waffle cookies—and that adds a great texture to the shell even after they're wrapped around the cannoli mold. These feel indulgent while at the same time seeming basic to any Italian family dinner. I often serve these for a birthday, anniversary, or holiday.

Homemade Cannoli

SERVES **12** HANDS-ON **1 HOUR**, **15 MINUTES**
TOTAL **2 HOURS**, **30 MINUTES**

1 Make the Cannoli Shells: Pulse the flour, sugar, salt, cinnamon, and baking soda in a food processor until combined, 5 to 6 times. Add the butter, and pulse until thoroughly combined, 3 to 4 times. Add the Marsala and egg yolk; process until the dough can be gently pressed into a ball, about 10 seconds. Turn the dough out onto a piece of plastic wrap, and shape into a flat disk. Let stand at room temperature for 1 hour.

2 Pour the oil to a depth of 2 inches into a large Dutch oven. Heat over medium to 350°F.

3 Meanwhile, roll half of the dough into a very thin circle on a lightly floured surface. Cut the dough with a 3½-inch round cutter; reroll the dough scraps once, and cut as many more circles as possible. Discard any remaining dough scraps. Repeat with remaining half of the dough.

4 Wrap 1 dough circle around each cannoli tube. Lightly moisten 1 edge with water, and press the edges together very firmly to seal. (If it is not well sealed, it will open during frying.) Fry the dough and cannoli tubes in the hot oil until golden brown, about 45 seconds. Using tongs, carefully remove from the hot oil. Remove the tubes from the shells, and place the shells on a paper towel-lined baking sheet to drain. Transfer to a wire rack, and cool completely, about 10 minutes. Repeat with remaining dough circles.

5 Make the Filling: Drain the ricotta in a fine wire-mesh strainer for about 30 minutes. Combine the drained ricotta, ¾ cup powdered sugar, orange zest, vanilla, and almond extract in a bowl; stir until smooth. Stir in the chocolate.

6 Spoon the ricotta mixture into a pastry bag fitted with a ¼-inch round tip. Pipe the ricotta mixture into the cannoli shells; arrange on a platter, and dust with the powdered sugar. Serve immediately.

CANNOLI SHELLS

2 cups all-purpose flour, plus more for work surface

2 tablespoons granulated sugar

½ teaspoon kosher salt

½ teaspoon ground cinnamon

¼ teaspoon baking soda

2 tablespoons cold unsalted butter, cut into small pieces

⅓ cup dry Marsala or white wine

1 large egg yolk

Vegetable oil

FILLING

2½ cups ricotta cheese

¾ cup powdered sugar, plus more for dusting

½ teaspoon orange zest

½ teaspoon vanilla extract

¼ teaspoon almond extract

⅓ cup grated bittersweet chocolate (about 1½ ounces), plus more for cannoli ends

◆ TRICK TECHNIQUE ◆

The best way to get chocolate shavings from a block of chocolate? Use your vegetable peeler.

PIZZELLES

⅔ cup all-purpose flour

6 tablespoons granulated sugar

2 tablespoons Dutch-process cocoa

2 teaspoons baking powder

¼ teaspoon kosher salt

¼ cup unsalted butter, melted

¼ cup whole milk

1 large egg

FILLING

2½ cups chopped fresh strawberries (about 14 ounces)

2 tablespoons granulated sugar

1½ tablespoons chopped fresh mint

7½ cups vanilla ice cream

MAKE AHEAD

The pizzelle shells can be made ahead and stored in an airtight container in the fridge for up to a week.

EQUIPMENT

You'll need a pizzelle maker for this recipe—but fear not! I provide another recipe or two for which you can use this specialty iron.

I know Neapolitan tacos sounds like an odd blend of cultures, but it will make perfect sense after this explanation. I have a thing about efficiency and value, and so I like when I can use seemingly specialized kitchen tools for more than their intended purpose, and such was the case with my pizzelle maker. I used it to make cookies. Check. Then one day I used it to make the cones for my ginger mousse, and in the midst of that production—and this will give you a good sense of the way my brain works—I thought, "Wait a minute! If I only folded the cone halfway, this would make a really good taco." I was right. The end result here are crispy, chocolaty, crunchy cookie shells that make the perfect host for creamy vanilla ice cream and minty macerated strawberries. As long as we're mixing cultures, I suggest serving these after grilling chicken and corn on the cob or hamburgers on a warm summer night. What's really neat is these look beautiful and are equally irresistible. No one can eat just one.

Neapolitan Tacos

SERVES **20**   HANDS-ON **40 MINUTES**   TOTAL **50 MINUTES**

1 Make the Pizzelles: Preheat a pizzelle maker according to the manufacturer's instructions. Whisk together the flour, sugar, cocoa, baking powder, and salt in a medium bowl. Whisk together the melted butter, milk, and egg in a small bowl; add to the flour mixture, and whisk until blended and smooth.

2 Coat the pizzelle maker with cooking spray. Spoon 1 tablespoon of the batter in the hot pizzelle maker; cook until set and slightly darker in color, 45 to 50 seconds. Use a small offset spatula to remove the pizzelles, and immediately drape the pizzelles over the handle of a wooden spoon (about ¾ inch to 1 inch in diameter) to form a taco shape; let stand until completely cool, about 3 minutes. Transfer to a wire rack, and repeat with remaining batter.

3 Make the Filling: Combine the strawberries, sugar, and mint in a medium bowl; let stand about 10 minutes, stirring occasionally to dissolve the sugar.

4 Spoon 3 small scoops of the vanilla ice cream (about 2 tablespoons per scoop) into each pizzelle taco; top each with about 1½ tablespoons of the strawberry mixture.

More frequently than you might imagine we will have guests over for an impromptu dinner and I'll need a quick, last-minute dessert. Do you know the drill? Rather than pull out store-bought cookies or a quart of old ice cream whose top is a layer of milky ice clusters from the last time we served it, I turn to this blueberry cheesecake. Every experienced home cook has a bag of tricks, and this is one of mine. My fridge always has mascarpone or ricotta cheese in it, and I always have frozen fruit and phyllo pastry shells in the freezer. The rest is as quick as the recipe claims. Mix the mascarpone with lemon zest and vanilla extract and voilà, cheese cake filling. Pipe that into the phyllo pastry shell, add a bit of fruit on top, and in an hour or less you have a party-worthy pickup dessert that's super simple, quick, and delicious.

Quick-and-Easy Blueberry Cheesecakes

SERVES **15**   HANDS-ON **15 MINUTES**   TOTAL **1 HOUR**

1 Preheat the oven to 400°F. Place the phyllo shells on a baking sheet and bake until golden brown, 5 to 7 minutes. Cool completely, about 15 minutes.

2 Beat the cream cheese, lemon zest, vanilla, and ¼ cup of the sugar with an electric mixer at medium speed until the mixture is smooth and the sugar dissolves, 1 to 2 minutes. Beat in the mascarpone until just blended. (Do not overbeat.) Spoon the mixture into a ziplock plastic bag; seal the bag, and snip about ½ inch from 1 corner of the bag. Pipe the mixture evenly into the phyllo shells (about 1½ teaspoons per shell).

3 Combine the blueberries, water, cinnamon, and remaining ¼ cup sugar in a small saucepan; bring to a simmer over medium, stirring constantly. Cook until the berries burst and the mixture is thickened, 5 to 8 minutes. Remove from the heat, and cool completely, about 20 minutes. Spoon the blueberry mixture over the cream cheese mixture in the phyllo shells. Cover and chill until ready to serve.

2 (1.9-ounce) packages frozen mini phyllo pastry shells, thawed

4 ounces cream cheese, softened

½ teaspoon lemon zest

½ teaspoon vanilla extract

½ cup granulated sugar

4 tablespoons mascarpone cheese, softened

1 cup fresh blueberries

1 tablespoon water

¼ teaspoon ground cinnamon

INGREDIENT NOTE

Mascarpone cheese, or Italian cream cheese, can be found at specialty markets. You could substitute crème fraîche in a pinch.

VARIATION

You could easily substitute raspberries or raspberry jam or chopped strawberries for the blueberries.

- 1 (16.5-ounce) package strawberry cake mix

- 1 (32-ounce) container part-skim ricotta cheese

- 2 (8-ounce) containers mascarpone cheese

- 4 large eggs

- ¾ cup granulated sugar

- 1 teaspoon vanilla extract

- 1 (3.4-ounce) package strawberry crème instant pudding mix

- 1 cup whole milk

I started making this cake in 2011 after my husband's father, Tony Vitale, began sending us issues of *La Gazzetta Italiana*, a wonderful little newspaper serving the Italian-American community in Cleveland. I always turned to the food section, and that February, I found a recipe for a Sicilian Chocolate Love Cake. I made it for a family Valentine's Day dinner and received a four-heart review. Everyone loved it. From there, I branched out. I made my favorite flavor, lemon, then on to butterscotch, and then one summer I tried strawberry, and that was the winner. The cake is moist, full of flavor, and I think the different layers make it look cool. If that isn't enough of an endorsement, I will simply say I *love* Italian Love Cake.

Strawberry Love Cake

SERVES **15**   HANDS-ON **20 MINUTES**   TOTAL **1 HOUR, 45 MINUTES**

1 Preheat the oven to 350°F. Grease and flour a 13- x 9-inch baking pan.

2 Prepare the cake mix according to the package directions; pour into the prepared baking pan, and set aside.

3 Beat the ricotta and 4 ounces of the mascarpone with an electric mixer at medium-low speed until smooth. Add the eggs, 1 at a time, beating just until combined after each addition. Add the sugar and vanilla, and beat until smooth. Gently spread the ricotta mixture evenly over the cake batter.

4 Bake until a wooden pick inserted in the center of the cake comes out clean and the strawberry layer has risen to the top, 50 to 60 minutes. Cool completely, about 30 minutes.

5 Meanwhile, beat the pudding mix and remaining 12 ounces mascarpone with an electric mixer at medium speed until smooth; gradually add the milk, beating until smooth. Let stand until thickened, about 5 minutes; spread the frosting over the cooled cake.

This English Lemon Cake is a wonderfully satisfying sweet after dinner and it's even better the next day as a lemony pick-me-up with my caffeine around 3 o'clock. That's the reason you're looking at this recipe right now. After getting home from meetings, I needed a cup of coffee and had a taste for something sweet. This cake was left over from dinner two nights before. It's my mom's recipe. (I had taken the actual recipe card from her collection.) Well, I took two bites and thought, I have to include this cake in my book. I'm sure there are people like me who occasionally want their cakes to do double duty—to score at dinner and be available for snacking the next day. Here it is. The reason this cake works is the pound-cake texture. It's delicious, with good lemon flavor and tasty almonds for a little crunch. Thanks, Mom!

English Lemon Cake

SERVES **12**   HANDS-ON **15 MINUTES**   TOTAL **2 HOURS, 40 MINUTES**

1   Preheat the oven to 350°F. Grease and flour a 10-inch tube pan. Beat the sugar and butter with an electric mixer at medium speed until light and fluffy, about 3 minutes. Add the eggs, 1 at a time, beating well after each addition. Whisk together the flour, baking powder, and salt in a separate bowl; add the flour mixture to the butter mixture alternately with the milk, beginning and ending with the flour mixture. Beat at low speed until blended after each addition, stopping to scrape the bowl as needed. Fold in the toasted almonds and the lemon zest. Pour the batter into the prepared pan.

2   Bake until the cake is golden brown and a wooden pick inserted in the center comes out clean, about 40 minutes. Cool in the pan for 15 minutes; remove the cake from the pan, and place on a wire rack. Brush the cake with the lemonade concentrate several times until absorbed. Cool completely, about 1½ hours. Sprinkle with the powdered sugar and extra lemon zest, and dollop with whipped cream, if desired, before serving.

2 cups granulated sugar

⅓ cup unsalted butter, plus more for pan

4 large eggs

3 cups all-purpose flour, plus more for pan

2 teaspoons baking powder

1 teaspoon kosher salt

1 cup whole milk

1 cup toasted slivered almonds

2 tablespoons lemon zest (from 2 lemons), plus more for garnish

¾ cup frozen lemonade concentrate, thawed, undiluted

Powdered sugar

Whipped cream (optional)

EQUIPMENT

You'll need a 10-inch tube pan for this recipe.

CARROT CAKE

3 cups grated carrots (from 4 medium carrots)

2 cups all-purpose flour, plus more for pan

2 cups granulated sugar

2 teaspoons baking soda

1 teaspoon baking powder

1 teaspoon ground cinnamon

½ teaspoon table salt

4 large eggs

1 cup vegetable oil

1 teaspoon vanilla extract

CREAM CHEESE FROSTING

1 (16-ounce) package powdered sugar

1 (8-ounce) package cream cheese, softened

½ cup unsalted butter, softened

1 cup pecans, chopped, plus more for cake

Carrot ribbons (optional)

◆ TRICK TECHNIQUE ◆

To make carrot ribbons, peel the carrots. Holding the carrot by the thicker end, slide the vegetable peeler away from you for thin ribbons. Continue to shave from the same place to get wide ribbons.

Like many people my age, I remember carrot cake popping up on menus and on our family's dinner table in the 1970s. Because of the carrots, I suppose, and the fruit used to sweeten and moisten the cake, it enjoyed the luster of healthiness, and that was and still is fine with me. I'll take a healthy cake any day. I'll tell you what else carrot cake had that others didn't—cream cheese frosting. Don't even look for health benefits here. From my very first bite, though, this cake became an exciting opportunity to enjoy this rich, creamy frosting—and the thicker it was spread on top the better it was. I often save a bite of two of just frosting for the end. This cake is moist and delicious, and leaving the sides uniced is a twist on the traditional, yet it's the way I remember my mom serving it when I was a kid. I serve this year-round and for the right person, someone like me, it can be a special birthday treat, too. It's also great with a cup of coffee.

Mom's Carrot Cake with Cream Cheese Frosting

SERVES 12   HANDS-ON 40 MINUTES   TOTAL 1 HOUR, 55 MINUTES

1 Make the Carrot Cake: Preheat the oven to 350°F. Line the bottoms of 3 greased and floured 9-inch round cake pans with parchment paper. Stir together the carrots, 2 cups of the flour, sugar, baking soda, baking powder, cinnamon, and salt; set aside.

2 Beat the eggs in a large bowl with an electric mixer at medium speed until smooth and thick, about 2 minutes. Add the oil and vanilla to the eggs; beat until combined. Gradually add the flour mixture to the egg mixture, beating well. Divide the batter evenly among the pans.

3 Bake until a wooden pick inserted in the center comes out clean, about 30 minutes. Cool in the pans for 15 minutes; remove from the pans, and cool completely on wire racks, about 30 minutes.

4 Make the Cream Cheese Frosting: Beat the powdered sugar, cream cheese, and butter with an electric mixer at medium speed until well blended; stir in the pecans. Spread the frosting between the layers and on the top of the cake. Top with the chopped pecans and the carrot ribbons, if desired.

If a cake can have an identity crisis, this is the one. Whenever I make this always well-received blueberry cake, a debate ensues between bites: Is it a cake? Or is it a cookie? This is because the cake is extremely dense and thick, as opposed to a traditional cake that is light and airy. Indeed, the first time I made this for some of the behind-the-scenes experts on my show, the notes they passed among themselves asked if I meant to do this—or was it a mistake. I explained I meant for it to be heavy and sweet, almost like a blueberry sugar cookie in cake form. I think the texture makes it equally nice for a luncheon dessert or afternoon cup of tea. I suggest dusting with powdered sugar at the end. If desired, a dollop of whipped cream is also a nice touch. Then, I leave it to you to decide: Is it a cake? Or a cookie?

Blueberry Cake

SERVES **8**   HANDS-ON **15 MINUTES**   TOTAL **1 HOUR, 20 MINUTES**

1 Preheat the oven to 350°F. Grease and flour an 8-inch springform pan. Whisk together 1 cup of the flour, baking powder, and salt.

2 Beat the granulated sugar, butter, and vanilla with an electric mixer at medium-high speed until light and fluffy, 3 to 5 minutes. Add the eggs, 1 at a time, beating until blended after each addition. Gradually add the flour mixture, beating at low speed until just blended. Spread the batter evenly in the prepared pan.

3 Combine the blueberries, lemon zest, lemon juice, cinnamon, and remaining 1 tablespoon flour; sprinkle the blueberry mixture evenly over the batter.

4 Bake until a wooden pick inserted in the center comes out clean, about 55 minutes. Cool in the pan about 10 minutes; run a thin knife around the edges of the cake. Remove the cake from the pan, and transfer to a platter. Dust the cake lightly with the powdered sugar. Serve warm or cool completely.

1 cup plus 1 tablespoon all-purpose flour, plus more for pan

1 teaspoon baking powder

½ teaspoon table salt

1 cup granulated sugar

½ cup unsalted butter, softened, plus more for pan

1 teaspoon vanilla extract

2 large eggs

2 cups fresh blueberries

1 teaspoon lemon zest, plus 1 teaspoon fresh lemon juice (from 1 lemon)

½ teaspoon ground cinnamon

Powdered sugar

EQUIPMENT

You'll need an 8-inch springform pan for this recipe.

2 cups packed light brown sugar

1 cup unsalted butter, softened

3 large eggs

3 cups all-purpose flour

2 teaspoons ground cinnamon

1 teaspoon baking soda

1 teaspoon baking powder

1 teaspoon ground allspice

¾ teaspoon kosher salt

½ teaspoon ground cloves

1 cup unsweetened applesauce

¾ cup raisins

½ cup chopped toasted pecans

Powdered sugar

EQUIPMENT

You'll need a 12-cup Bundt pan for this recipe.

Allspice. Cloves. Raisins. Pecans. Nuts and fruit. Around holiday time, these flavors start speaking to me. I think about them. I smell them. I taste them. I hear them urging me to use them in this delicious applesauce cake. This conversation between me and the sweeter things in life began when I was growing up. In addition to her Christmas cookies, my mom made this cake every time the holidays rolled around. I thought the inclusion of applesauce, one of my favorite sides at dinnertime, in a dessert was ingenious. For me, this cake has wonderful, warm memories, and it's provided the same to Tom's and my children. Now, it's part of our family holiday tradition. In a pinch, this is a special homemade gift to take to a festive potluck party.

Holiday Applesauce Cake

SERVES **12**   HANDS-ON **20 MINUTES**   TOTAL **1 HOUR, 25 MINUTES**

1 Preheat the oven to 350°F. Lightly grease a 12-cup Bundt pan with baking spray. Beat the sugar and butter with an electric mixer at medium speed until light and fluffy, 3 to 5 minutes. Add the eggs, 1 at a time, beating well after each addition. Whisk together the flour, cinnamon, baking soda, baking powder, allspice, salt, and cloves. Add the flour mixture and the applesauce alternately to the sugar mixture, beginning and ending with the flour mixture; beat at low speed until blended after each addition. Stir in the raisins and pecans. Pour the batter into the prepared pan.

2 Bake until a long wooden pick inserted in the center comes out clean, about 55 minutes. Cool in the pan about 10 minutes; remove from the pan, and cool completely on a wire rack. Dust the cake lightly with the powdered sugar before serving.

I'll give you the top three reasons I repeatedly turn to this cake. I love lemon curd. I love vanilla wafers. And I love how easy this is to make. In my house, this is a summertime cake when it's hot outside and I don't want to turn on the oven. After all the ingredients have been combined, the cake is refrigerated instead of baked, and I like that as much as I do the lemony tang of the curd and the cream cheese. If you're inclined, make your own lemon curd, but a store-bought jar is a perfect first option, as well as the kind of time-saver that makes this icebox cake super simple and satisfying. You can even whip this up a day or two ahead of time. Make it for a picnic, a potluck, or a chilled, refreshing treat for yourself.

Lemon Icebox Cake

SERVES **10**   HANDS-ON **20 MINUTES**
TOTAL **3 HOURS, 20 MINUTES, INCLUDING 3 HOURS CHILLING**

1 Beat the cream cheese and sugar with an electric mixer at medium speed until blended and smooth, 1 to 2 minutes. Add the cream, lemon zest, and vanilla; beat at medium-high speed just until stiff peaks form.

2 Arrange half of the cookies in a single layer on the bottom of a 13- x 9-inch baking dish, fitting in as many as possible without overlapping. Spoon half of the cream cheese mixture on top, and spread evenly with an offset spatula. Dollop ½ cup of the lemon curd by spoonfuls about 2 inches apart over the cream cheese mixture. Use a butter knife to swirl the curd into the cream cheese mixture. Top with remaining cookies and remaining cream cheese mixture. Dollop and swirl remaining lemon curd over the cream mixture. Cover with plastic wrap, and refrigerate until the cookies soften, about 3 hours.

4 ounces cream cheese, softened

⅓ cup powdered sugar

2½ cups heavy cream

2 teaspoons lemon zest (from 2 lemons)

½ teaspoon vanilla extract

1 (11-ounce) package vanilla wafers

1 cup Lemon Curd (page 29) or 1 (11.5-ounce) jar lemon curd

CRUST

1½ cups all-purpose flour, plus more for work surface and pan

1 cup almond flour

2 tablespoons granulated sugar

½ teaspoon kosher salt

½ teaspoon ground cinnamon

¾ cup cold unsalted butter, cut into pieces, plus more for pan

4 to 5 tablespoons ice-cold water

FILLING

2 (8-ounce) packages cream cheese, softened

½ cup granulated sugar

2 large eggs

½ teaspoon lemon zest, plus 1 tablespoon fresh lemon juice (from 1 lemon)

TOPPING

2 (10-ounce) packages frozen pitted dark sweet cherries, thawed

½ cup granulated sugar

1 teaspoon lemon zest, plus 2 tablespoons fresh lemon juice (from 1 lemon)

1 vanilla bean, split

⌐∘ VARIATION ∘⌐

You could easily substitute blueberries if you're not a cherry fan.

Ah, cheesecake. I like it in all shapes and flavors, but the tartness of cherries on top of a lemony filling makes every bite a sweet, lively celebration of favorite flavors. I think of this as pure comfort food, yet the pizza-thin quality of the crust keeps this on the lighter side and oh-so refreshing. My mom made many types of cakes, but I remember this particular cheesecake more often than any other, though I didn't make it for a long time. Then, a few years ago, my parents moved to a smaller house, and as we packed up their things, I found the 50-year-old pizza pan my mom used when she made her pie. Naturally, I took it home and made this recipe. There are a lot of steps. The crust must be prepared and chilled. The filling, though simple and quick, requires a taste or two in order to get the lemony zest forward enough. Finally, it must be baked and chilled again before you add the cherry topping. But none of it is difficult. And there's enough time between steps to work on the rest of your dinner. This is great for a group, especially one that prefers a light dessert.

Cherry Cheesecake Pizza Pie

SERVES **12**   HANDS-ON **40 MINUTES**   TOTAL **3 HOURS, 55 MINUTES**

1 Make the Crust: Process the all-purpose flour, almond flour, sugar, salt, and cinnamon in a food processor until combined, about 5 times. Add the butter, and pulse until the mixture is crumbly, 6 to 7 times. Add the water, 1 tablespoon at a time, pulsing just until the dough begins to form clumps. Shape the dough into a flat disk (about 1½ inches thick). Wrap with plastic wrap, and chill until firm, about 1 hour.

2 Preheat the oven to 350°F. Unwrap the dough, and roll into a 14-inch circle (about ¼ inch thick) on a lightly floured surface. Fit the dough into the bottom and up the sides of a greased and floured 12-inch tart pan with a removable bottom. Place the tart pan on a baking sheet; prick the dough with a fork. Line the dough with parchment paper or aluminum foil; fill with pie weights or dried beans.

3 Bake until the crust is set, about 25 minutes. Remove the pie weights and parchment, and cool completely. Leave the oven on.

4 Make the Filling: Beat the cream cheese and sugar with an electric mixer at medium speed until smooth. Add the eggs, 1 at a time, beating well after each addition. Beat in the lemon zest and lemon juice. Spread the cream cheese mixture into the cooled crust.

5 Bake until the cheesecake is set, about 25 minutes. Cool on a wire rack for 10 minutes. Place in the refrigerator, and chill until completely cool, about 45 minutes. Remove the cheesecake from the tart pan.

6 Make the Topping: Combine the cherries, sugar, lemon zest, and lemon juice in a medium saucepan over medium. Scrape the seeds from the vanilla bean, and add the seeds to the cherry mixture; discard the vanilla bean. Cook, stirring often, until the mixture is thick and syrupy, about 12 minutes. Remove from the heat, and cool 30 minutes. Spread the cherry mixture over the cheesecake.

Panna cotta sounds and tastes so decadent, and in the sense that it is an intensely thick, sweetened, and flavored cream, it is indulgent—but in the best possible way. Even better, you won't believe how simple this is to make or how it will melt in your mouth. Since panna cotta must chill and set for at least 8 hours, you can prepare it a day or two ahead and save yourself time, as you'll need to top it only with fresh fruit. I make this in the summer when the fruit is at its peak ripeness and plentiful.

Lemon-Raspberry Panna Cotta

SERVES **8**   HANDS-ON **15 MINUTES**   TOTAL **8 HOURS, 15 MINUTES, INCLUDING 8 HOURS CHILLING**

1 Combine the cream, milk, sugar, and lemon peel strips in a medium saucepan; bring just to a simmer over medium-high, stirring occasionally to dissolve the sugar. Remove from the heat, and let steep for 10 minutes, stirring occasionally.

2 Meanwhile, sprinkle the gelatin over the cold water in a small saucepan; let stand for 2 minutes. Cook over low just until the gelatin dissolves, about 2 minutes. Remove from the heat.

3 Stir the gelatin mixture into the cream mixture. Remove and discard the lemon peel strips. Divide the mixture among 8 (6-ounce) ramekins or custard cups. Cover and chill until set, at least 8 hours.

4 Dip the ramekins into a bowl of very hot water for about 5 seconds; run a thin knife or offset spatula around the outside of the custards, and invert onto serving plates. Top with the raspberries.

2 cups heavy cream

1 cup whole milk

½ cup granulated sugar

3 (3-inch) lemon peel strips

1 (¼-ounce) envelope unflavored gelatin

2 tablespoons cold water

1 cup small fresh raspberries

▷ VARIATION ◁

For variety, you can make this as a simple vanilla panna cotta, going heavier with the vanilla extract or vanilla bean paste instead of the lemon. You could also take advantage of seasonal fruit, such as peaches or nectarines, and add a few slices to the side of the plate as a garnish.

METRIC EQUIVALENTS

COOKING/OVEN TEMPERATURES

	Fahrenheit	Celsius	Gas Mark
Freeze Water	32° F	0° C	
Room Temp.	68° F	20° C	
Boil Water	212° F	100° C	
Bake	325° F	160° C	3
	350° F	180° C	4
	375° F	190° C	5
	400° F	200° C	6
	425° F	220° C	7
	450° F	230° C	8
Broil			Grill

LIQUID INGREDIENTS BY VOLUME

¼ tsp					=	1 ml		
½ tsp					=	2 ml		
1 tsp					=	5 ml		
3 tsp	=	1 Tbsp	=	½ fl oz	=	15 ml		
2 Tbsp	=	⅛ cup	=	1 fl oz	=	30 ml		
4 Tbsp	=	¼ cup	=	2 fl oz	=	60 ml		
5⅓ Tbsp	=	⅓ cup	=	3 fl oz	=	80 ml		
8 Tbsp	=	½ cup	=	4 fl oz	=	120 ml		
10⅔ Tbsp	=	⅔ cup	=	5 fl oz	=	160 ml		
12 Tbsp	=	¾ cup	=	6 fl oz	=	180 ml		
16 Tbsp	=	1 cup	=	8 fl oz	=	240 ml		
1 pt	=	2 cups	=	16 fl oz	=	480 ml		
1 qt	=	4 cups	=	32 fl oz	=	960 ml		
				33 fl oz	=	1000 ml	=	1 l

DRY INGREDIENTS BY WEIGHT

(To convert ounces to grams, multiply the number of ounces by 30.)

1 oz	=	1/16 lb	=	30 g
4 oz	=	¼ lb	=	120 g
8 oz	=	½ lb	=	240 g
12 oz	=	¾ lb	=	360 g
16 oz	=	1 lb	=	480 g

LENGTH

(To convert inches to centimeters, multiply inches by 2.5.)

1 in				=	2.5 cm		
12 in	=	1 ft		=	30 cm		
36 in	=	3 ft	=	1 yd	=	90 cm	
40 in	=			=	100 cm	=	1m

EQUIVALENTS FOR DIFFERENT TYPES OF INGREDIENTS

Standard Cup	Fine Powder (ex. flour)	Grain (ex. rice)	Granular (ex. sugar)	Liquid Solids (ex. butter)	Liquid (ex. milk)
1	140 g	150 g	190 g	200 g	240 ml
¾	105 g	113 g	143 g	150 g	180 ml
⅔	93 g	100 g	125 g	133 g	160 ml
½	70 g	75 g	95 g	100 g	120 ml
⅓	47 g	50 g	63 g	67 g	80 ml
¼	35 g	38 g	48 g	50 g	60 ml
⅛	18 g	19 g	24 g	25 g	30 ml

INDEX

ACKNOWLEDGMENTS

Like a restaurant serving a multicourse meal, a cookbook requires an assortment of wonderful, carefully selected fresh ingredients prepared, cooked, and served by a group of wonderful, carefully selected, extremely talented people, and that's exactly what I had in the making of this book, *Valerie's Home Cooking*. It's full of delicious recipes, generous tips, clever ideas, and beautiful photographs. I want to give thanks and credit to the people responsible, starting with my incredible editorial director Anja Schmidt and her equally incredible team: April Smitherman Colburn, Lacie Pinyan, Paden Reich, designer Allison Chi, Sue Chodakiewicz, Greg Amason, Donna Baldone, and Dolores Hydock. Then there are the photographers, prop stylists, food stylists, recipe testers, and recipe editors—there are too many of you to list in this short space, but please know that I know who you are, loved working with you, and appreciate the time, thought, and talent you put into this project. Thank you for giving me that part of your life. To my friends at the Food Network, and the production team and crew of my show *Valerie's Home Cooking,* you are the lemon zest in my life—and you know how much I love and crave and use my lemon zest. I also have a team of people who are essentials in my life. In food terms, you're the staples: Marc Schwartz, Jack Grossbart, Jill Fritzo, Jamie Mandelbaum, and Dan Strone. Thank you. I can't get this stuff done without you. Likewise, my assistant Jennifer Kramer. A huge thank you (and I didn't need you to schedule that—ha). And the same to my kooky, quirky, always-hungry, warm-hearted friend of 30-plus years, Todd Gold. Then there is my family: my son, my brothers and their wives and children, my stepchildren, and my husband, Tom (and let's not forget the big, passionate, food-loving family you brought into my world!). You are the sweet, the sour, and the spice in my life. All the best things. Hugs and kisses to you all. Finally, Mom and Dad—without you, there would be no home cooking in my life. There would be no me. And the same goes for Nonni and everyone who came before her. I'm the beneficiary of all your recipes and know-how, and more than anything else, the love you gave to me; very gratefully and appreciatively I'm able to share all of that with so many more people. With many thanks and much love, Valerie.